HEALING CRIMINAL †

The Ancient Egyptian Path of Redemption Through Virtue and Mystical Awakening
With complete guide to daily disciplines

by
Dr. Muata Ashby

Cruzian Mystic Books
P.O.Box 570459
Miami, Florida, 33257
(305) 378-6253 Fax: (305) 378-6253

First U.S. edition 1997
Second U.S. edition 1998
Third U.S. edition 2002
© 1997-1998-2002 By Reginald Muata Abhaya Ashby

The author is available for group lectures and individual counseling. For further information contact the publisher.

Ashby, Muata
Healing The Criminal Heart ISBN: 1-884564-17-8

Library of Congress Cataloging in Publication Data

1 Egyptian Mythology 2 Spirituality 3 Religion 4 Yoga 5 Self Help.

Also by Muata Ashby

Cruzian Mystic Books

Also by Muata Ashby

Resurrecting Osiris
The Story of Asar, Aset and Heru

For more listings see the back section.

Sema
Institute of Yoga

Sema (☥) is an ancient Egyptian word and symbol meaning *union*. The Sema Institute is dedicated to the propagation of the universal teachings of spiritual evolution which relate to the union of humanity and the union of all things within the universe. It is a non-denominational organization which recognizes the unifying principles in all spiritual and religious systems of evolution throughout the world. Our primary goals are to provide the wisdom of ancient spiritual teachings in books, courses and other forms of communication. Secondly, to provide expert instruction and training in the various yogic disciplines including Ancient Egyptian Philosophy, Christian Gnosticism, Indian Philosophy and modern science. Thirdly, to promote world peace and Universal Love.

A primary focus of our tradition is to identify and acknowledge the yogic principles within all religions and to relate them to each other in order to promote their deeper understanding as well as to show the essential unity of purpose and the unity of all living beings and nature within the whole of existence.

The Institute is open to all who believe in the principles of peace, non-violence and spiritual emancipation regardless of sex, race, or creed.

About the author and editor:
Dr. Muata Abhaya Ashby

About The Author

Reginald Muata Ashby holds a Doctor of Philosophy Degree in Religion, and a Doctor of Divinity Degree in Holistic Healing. He is also a Pastoral Counselor and Teacher of Yoga Philosophy and Discipline. Dr. Ashby is an adjunct faculty member of the American Institute of Holistic Theology and an ordained Minister. Dr. Ashby has studied advanced Jnana, Bhakti and Kundalini Yogas under the guidance of Swami Jyotirmayananda, a world renowned Yoga Master. He has studied the mystical teachings of ancient Egypt for many years and is the creator of the Egyptian Yoga concept. He is also the founder of the Sema Institute, an organization dedicated to the propagation of the teachings of Yoga and mystical spirituality.

Dr. Ashby began his research into the spiritual philosophy of Ancient Africa (Egypt) and India and noticed correlations in the culture and arts of the two countries. This was the catalyst for a successful book series on the subject called "Egyptian Yoga". Now he has created a series of musical compositions which explore this unique area of music from ancient Egypt and its connection to world music.

Karen Clarke-Ashby "Vijaya-Asha" is the wife and spiritual partner of Muata. She is an independent researcher, practitioner and certified teacher of Yoga, a Doctor in the Sciences and a Pastoral Counselor, the editor of Egyptian Proverbs and Egyptian Yoga by Muata.†

Sema Institute
P.O. Box 570459, Miami, Fla. 33257 (305) 378-6253,
Fax (305) 378-6253
©1997-2001

Table of Contents

About the sema Institute

Sema Institute-Temple of Aset

The term "Sma" (Sema, Sama) is a derivative of the term "Smai Tawi" meaning union of the Higher and lower Self, i.e. Yoga. Thus, The Sema Institute of Yoga, Temple of Aset, founded by Dr. Muata Ashby, Seba Maa ("Seba" is a Kamitan term that means spiritual preceptor and "Maa" is an abbreviation of the word "Maat") has as its sublime goal the dissemination of the Ancient Kamitan Teachings for the upliftment of humanity through the practice and attainment of Smai Taui (Divine Union). Its primary goals are: Firstly to provide the wisdom of ancient spiritual teachings in books, courses and other forms of communication. Secondly, to provide expert instruction and training in the various yogic disciplines including Kamitan (Ancient Egyptian) Religion and Mystical Philosophy, Christian Gnosticism, Indian Mysticism which are outgrowths of Kamitan Religion. Thirdly, to promote world peace and Universal Love. As Kamitan culture, from Africa, brought forth civilization, religion and mystical philosophy to the world, a primary focus of our tradition is to identify and acknowledge the Kamitan principles within all religions and to relate them to each other in order to promote their deeper understanding and show the essential unity. In our view, Kamitan Philosophy can be the foundation for the rebuilding of African culture and bridge the gap between religious differences, which will promote harmony and peace among peoples of differing creeds and ethnic backgrounds. The Institute is open to all that believe in the principles of peace, non-violence and spiritual emancipation regardless of sex, race, or creed. The Sema Institute is an organization, which recognizes the unifying principles in all spiritual and traditions throughout the world.

"Per Aset" means Temple of Aset. In Ancient times the Temple of Aset was a mecca for all mystics, saints and sages. It was a place where the disciplines of Smai Tawi was disseminated and practiced and its influence touched Ancient Greek culture and Ancient Roman culture as well as early Christianity. The Per Aset, now based in Miami, Florida, USA, follows the rediscovered disciplines of Kamitan Smai Tawi (Yoga) and teaches these through classes, worship services and publications.

Who is Seba Muata Abhaya Ashby D.D. Ph. D.?

Priest, Author, lecturer, poet, philosopher, musician, publisher, counselor and spiritual preceptor and founder of the Sema Institute-Temple of Aset, Muata Ashby was born in Brooklyn, New York City, and grew up in the Caribbean. His family is from Puerto Rico and Barbados. Displaying an interest in ancient civilizations and the Humanities, Seba Maa began studies in the area of religion and philosophy and achieved doctorates in these areas while at the same time he began to collect his research into what would later become several books on the subject of the origins of Yoga Philosophy and practice in ancient Africa (Ancient Egypt) and also the origins of Christian Mysticism in Ancient Egypt.

Seba Maa (Muata Abhaya Ashby) holds a Doctor of Philosophy Degree in Religion, and a Doctor of Divinity Degree in Holistic Health. He is also a Pastoral Counselor and Teacher of Yoga Philosophy and Discipline. Dr. Ashby received his Doctor of Divinity Degree from and is an adjunct faculty member of the American Institute of Holistic Theology. Dr. Ashby is a certified as a PREP Relationship Counselor. Dr. Ashby has been an independent researcher and practitioner of Egyptian Yoga, Indian Yoga, Chinese Yoga, Buddhism and mystical psychology as well as Christian Mysticism. Dr. Ashby has engaged in Post Graduate research in advanced Jnana, Bhakti and Kundalini Yogas at the Yoga Research Foundation. He has extensively studied mystical religious traditions from around the world and is an accomplished lecturer, musician, artist, poet, screenwriter, playwright and author of over 25 books on Kamitan yoga and spiritual philosophy. He is an Ordained Minister and Spiritual Counselor and also the founder the Sema Institute, a non-profit organization dedicated to spreading the wisdom of Yoga and the Ancient Egyptian mystical traditions. Further, he is the spiritual leader and head priest of the Per Aset or Temple of Aset, based in Miami, Florida. Thus, as a scholar, Dr. Muata Ashby is a teacher, lecturer and researcher. However, as a spiritual leader, his title is *Seba,* which means Spiritual Preceptor.

Seba Dr. Ashby began his research into the spiritual philosophy of Ancient Africa (Egypt) and India and noticed correlations in the culture and arts of the two countries. This was the catalyst for a successful book series on the subject called "Egyptian Yoga". Now he has created a series of musical compositions which explore this unique area of music from ancient Egypt and its connection to world music.

Who is Dr. Karen "Dja" Ashby?

Hemt Neter Karen Vijaya Clarke-Ashby is the wife and spiritual partner of Seba Dr. Muata Ashby as well as the vice-president of the Sema Institute-Temple of Aset. She a Kamitan Priestess (Hemt Neter) as well as an independent researcher, practitioner and teacher of Yoga, a Doctor in the Sciences, a Pastoral Counselor, and the editor of the Egyptian Yoga Book Series. Dr. Ashby has engaged in post-graduate research in advanced Jnana, Bhakti, Karma, Raja and Kundalini Yogas at the Yoga Research Foundation. She is a certified Yoga Exercise instructor, and a teacher of health and stress management uses of Yoga for modern society, based on the Kamitan and/or Indian yogic principles. Also, she is the co-author of *The Egyptian Yoga Exercise Workout Book*, contributing author on *The Kamitan Diet, Food for Body, Mind and Soul*, and author of Yoga Mystic Metaphors for Enlightenment.

Joining the Sema Institute or the Temple of Aset

The Institute holds regular classes, workshops, seminars around the country as well as internationally and study groups are being established nationally and internationally. For more information the reader may visit the Sema Institute – Per Aset Web Site at *www.Egyptianyoga.com*

Hotep -Peace be with you!
Seba Muata Ashby & Karen Ashby

Chapter 1: Brief History of Ancient Egypt

Temple of Aset (Egypt)

Where the Myth of Asar, Aset, and Heru was taught and studied in ancient times.

Who Were the Ancient Egyptians?

The Ancient Egyptian religion (*Shetaut Neter*), language and symbols provide the first "historical" record of Mystical Philosophy and Religious literature. Egyptian Mysticism is what has been commonly referred to by Egyptologists as Egyptian "Religion" or "Mythology," but to think of it as just another set of stories or allegories about a long lost civilization is to completely miss the greatest secret of human existence. Mystical spirituality, in all of its forms and disciplines of spiritual development, was practiced in Ancient Egypt (Kemet) earlier than anywhere else in history. This unique perspective from the highest philosophical system which developed in Africa over seven thousand years ago provides a new way to look at life, religion, the discipline of psychology and the way to spiritual development leading to spiritual Enlightenment. Ancient Egyptian mythology, when understood as a system of *Smai Tawi*, that is, a system which promotes the union of the individual soul with the Universal Soul or Supreme Consciousness, gives every individual insight into their own divine nature, and also a deeper insight into all religions, mystical and Yoga systems.

In Chapter 4 (Commonly referred to as Chapter 17) and Chapter 17 (Commonly referred to as Chapter 176) of an Ancient Egyptian mystical text, the *Prt m Hru, The Ancient Egyptian Book of Enlightenment*, more commonly known as the *Book of the Dead*, the term "Smai Tawi" is used. It means "Union of the two lands of Egypt." The two lands refers to the two main districts of the country (North and South) and, in a mystical sense they refer to the gods Heru and Set, who are elsewhere referred to as the spiritual Higher Self and lower self of a human being, respectively. Thus, the term Smai Tawi is compatible with the Indian Sanskrit term "Yoga," which also means union of the Higher Self and lower self as well as other terms (Enlightenment, Kingdom of Heaven, Liberation, etc.) used by other systems of mystical spirituality.

Diodorus Siculus (Greek Historian) writes in the time of Augustus (first century B.C.):

"Now the Ethiopians, as historians relate, were the first of all men and the proofs of this statement, they say, are manifest. For that they did not come into their land as immigrants from abroad, but were the natives of it and so justly bear the name of autochthones (sprung from the soil itself), is, they maintain, conceded by practically all men..."

"They also say that the Egyptians are colonists sent out by the Ethiopians, Asar having been the leader of the colony. For, speaking generally, what is now Egypt, they maintain, was not land, but sea, when in the beginning the universe was being formed; afterwards, however, as the Nile during the times of its inundation carried down the mud from Ethiopia, land was gradually built up from the deposit...And the larger parts of the customs of the Egyptians are, they hold, Ethiopian, the colonists still preserving their ancient manners. For instance, the belief that their kings are Gods, the very special attention which they pay to their burials, and many other matters of a similar nature, are Ethiopian practices, while the shapes of their statues and the forms of their letters are Ethiopian; for of the two kinds of writing which the Egyptians have, that which is known as popular (demotic) is learned by everyone, while that which is called sacred (hieratic), is understood only by the priests of the Egyptians, who learnt it from their Fathers as one of the things which are not divulged, but among the Ethiopians, everyone uses these forms of letters. Furthermore, the orders of the priests, they maintain, have much the same position among both peoples; for all are clean who are engaged in the service of the gods, keeping themselves shaven, like the Ethiopian priests, and having the same dress and form of staff, which is shaped like a plough and is carried by their kings who wear high felt hats which end in a knob in the top and are circled by the serpents which they call asps; and this symbol appears to carry the thought that it will be the lot who shall dare to attack the king to encounter death-carrying stings. Many other things are told by them concerning their own antiquity and the colony which they sent out that became the Egyptians, but about this there is no special need of our writing anything."

The Ancient Egyptian texts state:

"Our people originated at the base of the mountain of the Moon, at the origin of the Nile river."

The ancient name for the land now called Egypt was:

"KMT" "Egypt," "Burnt," "Black people," "Black Land"

The World

Below: Map of the world showing
the scope of Ancient Egyptian culture in ancient times.

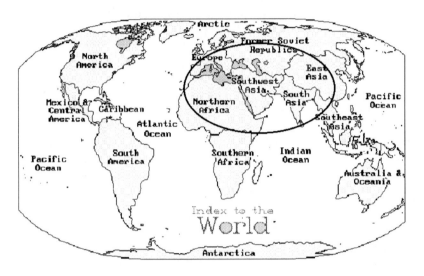

In describing the Ancient Egyptians of his time Herodotus (Greek historian c. 484-425 BC), said: *"The Egyptians and Nubians have thick lips, broad noses, wooly hair and burnt skin... ...And the Indian tribes I have mentioned, their skins are all of the same color, much like the Ethiopians... their country is a long way from Persia towards the south..."* Diodorus, the Greek historian (c. 100 B.C.) said the following, *"And upon his return to Greece, they gathered around and asked, "tell us about this great land of the Blacks called Ethiopia." And Herodotus said, "There are two great Ethiopian nations, one in Sind (India) and the other in Egypt."* Thus, the Ancient Egyptian peoples were of African origin and they had close ties in ancient times with the peoples of India.

Where is the land of Ancient Egypt?

A map of North East Africa showing the location of the land of *Ta-Meri* or *Kamit,* also known as Ancient Egypt.

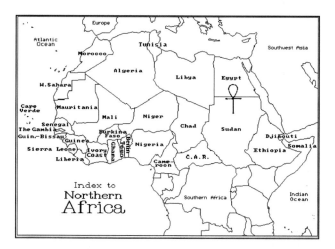

The Ancient Egyptians lived for thousands of years in the northeastern corner of the African continent in the area known as the Nile Valley. The Nile river was a source of dependable enrichment for the land and allowed them to prosper for a very long time. Their prosperity was so great that they created art, culture, religion, philosophy and a civilization which has not been duplicated since. The Ancient Kamitans (Egyptians) based their government and business concerns on spiritual values and therefore, enjoyed an orderly society which included equality between the sexes, and a legal system based on universal spiritual laws. The *Prt m Hru* is a tribute to their history, culture and legacy. As historical insights unfold, it becomes clearer that modern culture has derived its basis from Ancient Egypt, though the credit is not often given, nor the integrity of the practices maintained. This is another important reason to study Ancient Egyptian Philosophy, to discover the principles which allowed their civilization to prosper over a period of thousands of years in order to bring our systems of government, religion and social structures to a harmony with ourselves, humanity and with nature.

Christianity was partly an outgrowth of Judaism, which was itself an outgrowth of Ancient Egyptian culture and religion. So who were the Ancient Egyptians? From the time that the early Greek philosophers set foot on African soil to study the teachings of mystical spirituality in Egypt (900-300 B.C.E.), Western society and culture was forever changed. Ancient Egypt had such a profound effect on Western civilization as well as on the native population of Ancient India (Dravidians) that it is important to understand the history and culture of Ancient Egypt, and the nature of its spiritual tradition in more detail.

When Was Neterian Religion Practiced?

The history of Egypt begins in the far reaches of history. It includes The Dynastic Period, The Hellenistic Period, Roman and Byzantine Rule (30 B.C.E.-638 A.C.E.), the Caliphate and the Mamalukes (642-1517 A.C.E.), Ottoman Domination (1082-1882 A.C.E.), British colonialism (1882-1952 A.C.E.), as well as modern, Arab-Islamic Egypt (1952- present).

Ancient Egypt or Kamit had a civilization that flourished in Northeast Africa along the Nile River from before 5,500 B.C.E. until 30 B.C.E. In 30 B.C.E., Octavian, who was later known as the Roman Emperor, Augustus, put the last Egyptian King, Ptolemy XIV, a Greek ruler, to death. After this Egypt was formally annexed to Rome. Egyptologists normally divide Ancient Egyptian history into the following approximate periods: The Early Dynastic Period (3,200-2,575 B.C.E.); The Old Kingdom or Old Empire (2,575-2,134 B.C.E.); The First Intermediate Period (2,134-2,040 B.C.E.); The Middle Kingdom or Middle Empire (2,040-1,640 B.C.E.); The Second Intermediate Period (1,640-1,532 B.C.E.); The New Kingdom or New Empire (1,532-1,070 B.C.E.); The third Intermediate Period (1,070-712 B.C.E.); The Late Period (712-332 B.C.E.).

In the Late Period the following groups controlled Egypt. The Nubian Dynasty (712-657 B.C.E.); The Persian Dynasty (525-404 B.C.E.); The Native Revolt and re-establishment of Egyptian rule by Egyptians (404-343 B.C.E.); The Second Persian Period (343-332 B.C.E.); The Ptolemaic or Greek Period (332 B.C.E.- c. 30 B.C.E.); Roman Period (c.30 B.C.E.-395 A.C.E.); The Byzantine Period (395-640 A.C.E) and The Arab Conquest Period (640 A.C.E.-present). The individual dynasties are numbered, generally in Roman numerals, from I through XXX.

The period after the New Kingdom saw greatness in culture and architecture under the rulership of Ramses II. However, after his rule, Egypt saw a decline from which it would never recover. This is the period of the downfall of Ancient Egyptian culture in which the Libyans ruled after The Tanite (XXI) Dynasty. This was followed by the Nubian conquerors who founded the XXII dynasty and tried to restore Egypt to her past glory. However, having been weakened by the social and political turmoil of wars, Ancient Egypt fell to the Persians once more. The Persians conquered the country until the Greeks, under Alexander, conquered them. The Romans followed the Greeks, and finally the Arabs conquered the land of Egypt in 640 A.C.E to the present.

However, the history which has been classified above is only the history of the "Dynastic Period." It reflects the view of traditional Egyptologists who have refused to accept the evidence of a Predynastic period in Ancient Egyptian history contained in Ancient Egyptian documents such as the *Palermo Stone, Royal Tablets at Abydos, Royal Papyrus of Turin*, the *Dynastic List* of *Manetho*. The eye-witness accounts of Greek historians Herodotus (c. 484-425 B.C.E.) and Diodorus (Greek historian died about 20 B.C.E.) corroborate the status and makeup of Kamitan culture in the late dynastic period which support the earlier accounts. These sources speak clearly of a Pre-dynastic society which stretches far into antiquity. The Dynastic Period is what most people think of whenever Ancient Egypt is mentioned. This period is when the pharaohs (kings) ruled. The latter part of the Dynastic Period is when the Biblical story of Moses, Joseph, Abraham, etc., occurs (c. 2100? -1,000? B.C.E). Therefore, those with a Christian background generally only have an idea about Ancient Egypt as it is related in the Bible. Although this biblical notion is very limited in scope, the significant impact of Ancient Egypt on Hebrew and Christian culture is evident even from the biblical scriptures. Actually, Egypt existed much earlier than most traditional Egyptologists are prepared to admit. The new archeological evidence related to the great Sphinx monument on the Giza Plateau and the ancient writings by Manetho, one of the last High Priests of Ancient Egypt, show that Ancient Egyptian history begins earlier than 10,000 B.C.E. and may date back to as early as 30,000-50,000 B.C.E.

It is known that the Pharaonic (royal) calendar based on the Sothic system (star Sirius) was in use by 4,240 B.C.E. This certainly required extensive astronomical skills and time for observation. Therefore, the history of Kamit (Egypt) must be reckoned to be extremely ancient. Thus, in order to grasp the antiquity of Ancient Egyptian culture, religion and philosophy, we will briefly review the history presented by the Ancient Egyptian Priest Manetho and some Greek Historians.

The calendar based on the Great Year was also used by the Ancient Egyptians. The Great year is based on the movement of the earth through the constellations known as the precession of the Equinoxes and confirmed by the History given by the Ancient Egyptian Priest Manetho in the year 241 B.C.E. Each Great Year has 25,860 to 25,920 years and 12 arcs or constellations, and each passage through a constellation takes 2,155 – 2,160 years. These are the "Great Months." The current cycle or year began around the year 10,858 B.C.E. At around the year 36,766 B.C.E., according to Manetho, the Creator, Ra, ruled the earth in person from his throne in the Ancient Egyptian city of Anu. By this reckoning our current year (2,000 A.C.E.) is actually the year 38,766 based on the Great Year System of Ancient Egyptian history.

Below left: A map of North East Africa showing the location of the land of *Ta-Meri* or *Kamit,* also known as Ancient Egypt and South of it is located the land which in modern times is called Sudan.

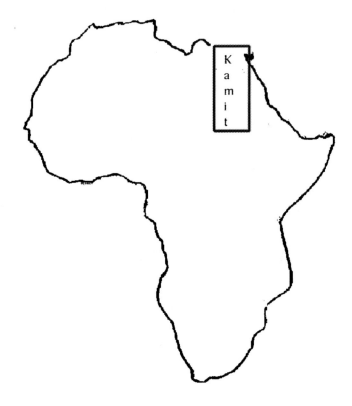

Healing the Criminal Heart

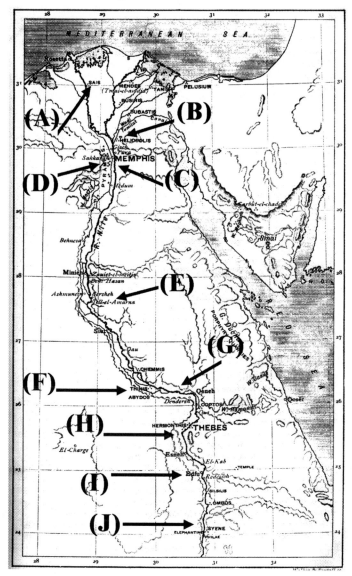

Above right- The Land of Ancient Egypt-Nile Valley and major cities in ancient times.

The cities wherein the theology of the Trinity of Amun-Ra-Ptah was developed were: A- Sais (temple of Net), B- Anu (Heliopolis- temple of Ra), C-Men-nefer or Hetkaptah (Memphis, temple of Ptah), and D- Sakkara (Pyramid Texts), E- Akhet-Aton (City of Akhnaton, temple of Aton), F- Abdu (temple of Asar), G- Denderah (temple of Hetheru), H- Waset (Thebes, temple of Amun), I- Edfu (temple of Heru), J- Philae (temple of Aset). The cities wherein the theology of the Trinity of Asar-Aset-Heru was developed were Anu, Abydos, Philae, Denderah and Edfu.

19

The Two Lands of Egypt

In Chapter 4 (Commonly referred to as Chapter 17) and Chapter 17(Commonly referred to as Chapter 176) of the Ancient Egyptian mystical text, the *Prt m Hru, The Ancient Egyptian Book of Enlightenment*, more commonly known as the *Book of the Dead,* the term "Smai Tawi" is used. It means "Union of the two lands of Egypt." The two lands refers to the two main districts of the country (North and South) and, in a mystical sense they refer to the gods Heru (the north) and Set (the south land), who are elsewhere referred to as the spiritual Higher Self and lower self of a human being, respectively. Thus, the term Smai Tawi is compatible with the Indian Sanskrit term "Yoga," which also means union of the Higher Self and lower self as well as other terms (enlightenment, Kingdom of Heaven, Liberation, etc.) used by other systems of mystical spirituality.

Diodorus Siculus (Greek Historian) writes in the time of Augustus (first century B.C.):

> "Now the Ethiopians, as historians relate, were the first of all men and the proofs of this statement, they say, are manifest. For that they did not come into their land as immigrants from abroad, but were the natives of it and so justly bear the name of autochthones (sprung from the soil itself), is, they maintain, conceded by practically all men..."

> "They also say that the Egyptians are colonists sent out by the Ethiopians, Asar having been the leader of the colony. For, speaking generally, what is now Egypt, they maintain, was not land, but sea, when in the beginning the universe was being formed; afterwards, however, as the Nile during the times of its inundation carried down the mud from Ethiopia, land was gradually built up from the deposit...And the larger parts of the customs of the Egyptians are, they hold, Ethiopian, the colonists still preserving their ancient manners. For instance, the belief that their kings are Gods, the very special attention which they pay to their burials, and many other matters of a similar nature, are Ethiopian practices, while the shapes of their statues and the forms of their letters are Ethiopian; for of the two kinds of writing which the Egyptians have, that which is known as popular (demotic) is learned by everyone, while that which is called sacred (hieratic), is understood only by the priests of the Egyptians, who learnt it from their Fathers as one of the things which are not divulged, but among the Ethiopians, everyone uses these forms of letters. Furthermore, the orders of the priests, they maintain, have much the same position among both peoples; for all are clean who are engaged in the service of the gods, keeping themselves shaven, like the Ethiopian priests, and having the same dress and form of staff, which is shaped like a plough and is carried by their kings who wear high felt hats which end in a knob in the top and are circled by the serpents which they call asps; and this

symbol appears to carry the thought that it will be the lot who shall dare to attack the king to encounter death-carrying stings. Many other things are told by them concerning their own antiquity and the colony which they sent out that became the Egyptians, but about this there is no special need of our writing anything."

How Some Western and Arab Scholars Distort Evidence Pointing to the Older Age of Ancient Egyptian Culture

After examining the writings of many Western scholars the feeling by many Afrocentrists and Africologists (researchers into African culture) of African descent and some western scholars, is that traditional Egyptologists, a group composed almost entirely of people of European descent or trained by western scholars, have over the years sought to bring down the estimated date for the commencement of the dynastic period in Egypt in order to show that Ancient Egyptian culture emerged after Mesopotamian culture. Presumably, this was done because Mesopotamia is held by many Western scholars to be their (Western Culture's) own, if not genetic, cultural ancestral homeland. The reader should understand the context of this issue which goes to the heart of cultural relations between Western culture and Eastern and African cultures. From the perspective of many people of non-European descent they see a culture which has sought to establish its socio-economic supremacy by suppressing and undermining the capacity of indigenous peoples to govern themselves and control their own resources. This is verified by the documented evidence of the African slave trade, (*The Middle Passage : White Ships Black Cargo* by Tom Feelings, John Henrik, Dr Clarke) military and covert intervention to destabilize governments, distortion of history, (**Stolen Legacy**, George James \ *Black Athena, The Afroasiatic Origins of Classical Civilization* by Martin Bernal) colonial and neocolonial systems, (***Destruction of Black Civilization: Great Issues of a Race from 4500bc to 2000ad*** by Chancellor Williams) etc., either set up or supported by Western countries in the past 500 years. In order to perpetuate this control the image of superiority demands that Western culture should be able to project an ancestral right as it were to control other countries. Therefore, twisting evidence in order to make Western culture appear ancient, wise, beneficial, etc., necessitates a denial that there is any civilization that is older or at least better than Western civilization or that there could be any genetic or cultural relation with non-western cultures which are being subjugated and thereby a common ancestry with the rest of humanity. An example of this twisting of history by Western scholars is the well known and documented deliberate misinterpretation of the Bible story of Noah so as to make it appear that the Bible advocated and condones the enslavement of the children (descendants) of Ham (all Hamitic peoples- people of African descent) by the children (descendants) of Japheth (all peoples of Germanic (European) descent).

Genesis 9:26-27:

26 And he said, Blessed [be] the LORD God of Shem; and Canaan shall be his servant. {his servant: or, servant to them}

27 God shall enlarge Japheth, and he shall dwell in the tents of
Shem; and Canaan shall be his servant. {enlarge: or, persuade}

The perceived continued denial of the past and the continued process of
benefiting from past wrongdoing is a strong concern for many people around the
world who feel they have been misled, abused by Western culture. A case often cited
is distortion of the biblical story of Ham. In the Bible itself there is an attempt to
show that the main Jewish ancestors comes from the blood-line of Shem (Genesis
11:10-26). This is done in an effort to follow up on the idea given in Genesis 9:26-
27, that the Canaanites should be serving the Jews. These Biblical statements, like
"be fruitful and multiply" (Genesis 1:28) and other "commands" of God are in reality
mandates or directives written into the Bible for guiding the goals and objectives of
the Jews. They are similar to political edicts, and acted to reinforce a particular
agenda for the masses of people to believe in and pursue. They give a purpose and
meaning to the lives of the Jews but they are not to be understood as spiritual edicts
to be followed literally. They were written for a certain time and purpose which is
several thousands of years removed from the present.

The Far Reaching Implications of the New Evidence Concerning the Sphinx and Other New Archeological Evidence in Egypt and the Rest of Africa

In the last 20 years traditional Egyptologists, archeologists and others have been
taking note of recent studies performed on the Ancient Egyptian Sphinx which sits at
Giza in Egypt. Beginning with such students of Ancient Egyptian culture and
architecture as R. A. Schwaller de Lubicz in the 1950's, and most recently, John
Anthony West, with his book *Serpent In the Sky*, many researchers have used modern
technology to study the ancient monument and their discoveries have startled the
world. They now understand that the erosion damage on the Sphinx could not have
occurred after the period 10,000-7,000 B.C.E. because this was the last period in
which there would have been enough rainfall in the area to cause such damage. This
means that most of the damage which the Sphinx displays itself, which would have
taken thousands of years to occur, would have happened prior to that time (10,000
B.C.E.).

Many scholars have downplayed or misunderstood the new geological evidences
related to the Great Sphinx. One example are the authors of the book *In Search of the
Cradle of Civilization,* Georg Feuerstein, David Frawley (prominent western
Indologists), and Subhash Kak, in which the authors state the following: (highlighted
text is by Ashby)

> In seeking to refute current archeological thinking about the Sphinx,
> West relies on a *single geological feature*. Understandably, most
> Egyptologists have been less than accepting of his redating of this

monument, *hoping* that some other explanation can be found for the *strange* marks of erosion. P. 6

The characterization of the evidence as a "single geological feature" implies it stands alone as an anomaly that does not fit into the greater picture of Ancient Egyptian history and is completely without basis. In support of orthodox Egyptologists, the authors agree with them, stating that their attitude is understandable. Now, even if there were only a single form of evidence, does this mean that it is or should be considered suspect especially when considering the fact that Egyptology and archeology are not exact sciences and geology is an exact science? Further, the authors mention the wishful thinking of the orthodox Egyptologists as they search in vein (hoping) for some other way to explain the evidence. Yet, the authors seem to agree with the Egyptological view and thereby pass over this evidence as an inconsistency that need not be dealt with further.

> The following evidences must also be taken into account when examining the geology of the Sphinx and the Giza plateau.

> ➤ The surrounding Sphinx Temple architecture is similarly affected.

> ➤ Astronomical evidence agrees with the geological findings.

> ➤ Ancient Egyptian historical documents concur with the evidence.

It is important to understand that what we have in the Sphinx is not just a monument now dated as the earliest monument in history (based on irrefutable geological evidence). Its existence signifies the earliest practice not only of high-art and architecture, but it is also the first monumental statue in history dedicated to religion. This massive project including the Sphinx and its attendant Temple required intensive planning and engineering skill. Despite its deteriorated state, the Sphinx stands not only as the most ancient mystical symbol in this historical period, but also as the most ancient architectural monument, and a testament to the presence of Ancient African (Egyptian) culture in the earliest period of antiquity. Further, this means that while the two other emerging civilizations of antiquity (Sumer and Indus) were in their Neolithic period (characterized by the development of agriculture, pottery and the making of polished stone implements), Ancient Egypt had already achieved mastery over monumental art, architecture and religion as an adjunct to social order, as the Sphinx is a symbol of the Pharaoh (leader and upholder of Maat-order, justice and truth) as the god Heru. The iconography of the Sphinx is typical of that which is seen throughout Ancient Egyptian history and signals the achievement of the a culture of high morals which governs the entire civilization to the Persian and Greek conquest.

Plate 1: The Great Sphinx of Ancient Egypt-showing the classical Pharaonic headdress popularized in Dynastic times. Also, the water damage can be seen in the form of vertical indentations in the sides of the monument.

> The water erosion of the Sphinx is to history what the convertibility of matter into energy is to physics.
>
> -John Anthony West *Serpent In the Sky*

Many people have heard of the new evidence concerning the water damage on the Sphinx and how it has been shown to be much older than previously thought. However, as we saw earlier, detractors usually claim that this is only one piece of evidence that is inconclusive. This is the usual opinion of the uninformed. The findings have been confirmed by seismographic tests (*Traveler's Key to Ancient Egypt*, John Anthony West) as well as examination of the water damage on the structures related to the Sphinx and the Sphinx Temple, as compared to the rest of the structures surrounding it which display the typical decay due to wind and sand. It has been conclusively found that the Sphinx and its adjacent structures (Sphinx Temple) were built in a different era and that the surrounding structures do not display the water damage. Therefore, the wind and sand damaged structures belong to the Dynastic Era and the Sphinx belongs to the Pre-Dynastic Era. Therefore, the evidence supporting the older dating of the Sphinx is well founded and confirmed.

Plate 2: Sphinx rump and Sphinx enclosure show detail of the water damage (vertical damage).

The new evidence related to the Sphinx affects many other forms of evidence which traditional Egyptologists have also sought to dismiss. Therefore, it is a momentous discovery on the order the discernment of the Ancient Egyptian Hieroglyphic text. It requires an opening up of the closely held chronologies and timelines of ancient cultures for revision, thereby allowing the deeper study of the human experience on this earth and making the discovery of our collective past glory possible. Thus, it is clear to see that the problem in assigning dates to events in Ancient Egypt arises when there is an unwillingness to let go of closely held notions based on biased information that is accepted as truth and passed on from one generation of orthodox Egyptologists to the next generation, rather than on authentic scholarship (constant search for truth). This deficiency led to the exclusion of the ancient historical writings of Ancient Egypt (*Palermo Stone, Royal Tablets at Abydos, Royal Papyrus of Turin,* the *Dynastic List* of Manetho). However, now, with the irrefutable evidence of the antiquity of the Sphinx, and the excavations at Abydos and Hierakonpolis, the mounting archeological evidence and the loosening grip of Western scholars on the field of Egyptology, it is no longer possible to ignore the far reaching implications of the Ancient Egyptian historical documents.

Who Were the Ancient Egyptians and What is Yoga Philosophy?

A Long History

For a period spanning over 10,000 years the Neterian religion served the society of ancient Kamit. It is hard to comprehend the vastness of time that is encompassed by Ancient Egyptian culture, religion and philosophy. Yet the evidence is there to be seen by all. It has been collected and presented in the book *African Origins of Civilization, Religion and Yoga Philosophy.* That volume will serve as the historical record for the Neterian religion and as record of its legacy to all humanity. It serves as the basis or foundation for the work contained in all the other books in this series that have been created to elucidate on the teachings and traditions as well as disciplines of the varied Neterian religious traditions.

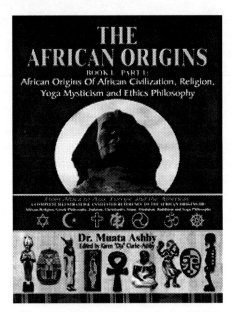

The book *African Origins of Civilization, Religion and Yoga Philosophy,* and the other volumes on the specific traditions detail the philosophies and disciplines that should be practiced by those who want to follow the path of Hm or Hmt, to be practitioners of the Shetaut Neter religion and builders of the Neterian faith worldwide. Below is a summary of the findings contained in the book African Origins in relations to the subject of the ancient historical dating of Ancient Egyptian civilization.

Chapter 2: Culture of the Ancient Kamitans

An Ancient Egyptian Man

The Ancient Egyptian (Kamitic) religion (*Shetaut Neter*), language and symbols provide the first "historical" record of Mystical Philosophy and Religious literature. Egyptian Mysticism is what has been commonly referred to by Egyptologists as Egyptian "Religion" or "Myth," but to think of it as just another set of stories or allegories about a long lost civilization is to completely miss the greater teaching it has to offer. Mystical spirituality, in all of its forms and disciplines of spiritual development, was practiced in Ancient Egypt (Kemet) earlier than anywhere else in history. This unique perspective from the highest philosophical system which developed in Africa over seven thousand years ago provides a new way to look at life, religion, the discipline of psychology and the way to spiritual development leading to spiritual Enlightenment. Ancient Egyptian myth, when understood as a system of *Smai Tawi* (Egyptian Yoga), that is, a system which promotes the union of the individual soul with the Universal Soul or Supreme Consciousness, gives every individual insight into their own divine nature, and also a deeper insight into all religions, mystical and Yoga systems.

Ancient Egyptian culture and philosophy is crucial to the understanding of world history and spirituality. It is especially important for people of African descent to know and understand their roots and thereby become powerful and dynamic members of the world community. The study of Kamitan Spirituality is also important for people of Indian descent as they too share in the Kamitan legacy. This knowledge will allow them to understand the depth of their own culture and spiritual tradition as well as aid in the restoration of positive interactions with people of African descent and Africa itself.

The Term Kamit and the Origins of the Ancient Egyptians

The Ancient Egyptians recorded that they were originally a colony of Ethiopians from the south who came to the north east part of Africa. The term "Ethiopian," "Nubian," and "Kushite" all relate to the same peoples who lived south of Egypt. In modern times, the land which was once known as Nubia ("Land of Gold"), is currently known as the Sudan, and the land even further south and east towards the coast of east Africa is referred to as Ethiopia (see map above).

Recent research has shown that the modern Nubian word *kiji* means "fertile land, dark gray mud, silt, or black land." Since the sound of this word is close to the Ancient Egyptian name Kish or Kush, referring to the land south of Egypt, it is believed that the name Kush also meant "the land of dark silt" or "the black land." Kush was the Ancient Egyptian name for Nubia. Nubia, the black land, is the Sudan of today. Sudan is an Arabic translation of *sûd* which is the plural form of *aswad*, which means "black," and *ân* which means "of the." So, Sudan means "of the blacks." In the modern Nubian language, *nugud* means "black." Also, *nuger*, *nugur*, and *nubi* mean "black" as well. All of this indicates that the words Kush, Nubia, and Sudan all mean the same thing — the "black land" and/or the "land of the blacks." As we will see, the differences between the term Kush and the term Kam (Qamit -

name for Ancient Egypt in the Ancient Egyptian language) relate more to the same meaning but different geographical locations.

As we have seen, the terms "Ethiopia," "Nubia," "Kush" and "Sudan" all refer to "black land" and/or the "land of the blacks." In the same manner we find that the name of Egypt which was used by the Ancient Egyptians also means "black land" and/or the "land of the blacks." The hieroglyphs below reveal the Ancient Egyptian meaning of the words related to the name of their land. It is clear that the meaning of the word Qamit is equivalent to the word Kush as far as they relate to "black land" and that they also refer to a differentiation in geographical location, i.e. Kush is the "black land of the south" and Qamit is the "black land of the north." Both terms denote the primary quality that defines Africa, "black" or "Blackness" (referring to the land and its people). The quality of blackness and the consonantal sound of K or Q as well as the reference to the land are all aspects of commonality between the Ancient Kushitic and Kamitan terms.

As we have seen, the terms "Ethiopia," "Nubia," "Kush" and "Sudan" which all refer to "black land" and/or the "land of the blacks." In the same manner we find that the name of Egypt which was used by the Egyptians also means "black land" and/or the "land of the blacks." The hieroglyphs below reveal the Ancient Egyptian meaning of the words related to the name of their land.

 Qamit - Ancient Egypt

Qamit - blackness – black

Qamit - literature of Ancient Egypt – scriptures

Qamiu - Ancient Egyptians-people of the black land

"QMT" (KMT, Kemet, Kamit), "Egypt," "Burnt," "Black people," "Black Land"

The African Ancestry of the Ancient Egyptians

Many of the same writers who lived in the times of the Ancient Egyptians described them and confirmed that they were of African descent. Some of the descriptions state that they had wooly hair and were burnt (black) of skin. Some say that they also had thick lips as the Ethiopians and other Africans. This shows that the Ancient Egyptian Philosophy, though universal in its scope, is a creation of ancient African peoples. Who did not hoard their wisdom but shared it freely with the world. This is a matter of truth which must be affirmed whenever the origins of the teachings is discussed. It underscores the African contributions to the emergence of western culture and modern civilization.

> "...several Egyptians told me that in their opinion the Colchidians were descended from soldiers of Sesotris. I had conjectured as much myself from two pointers, firstly because **they have black skins and kinky hair...**and more reliably for the reason that alone among mankind the Egyptians and the Ethiopian have practiced circumcision since time immemorial." (Herodotus, Book II, 104)

> "The **Egyptians and Nubians have thick lips, broad noses, wooly hair and burnt skin...**
> ...And the Indian tribes I have mentioned, their skins are all of the same color, much like the Ethiopians... their country is a long way from Persia towards the south..."
>
> Herodotus

> "And upon his return to Greece, they gathered around and asked, "tell us about this great **land of the Blacks called Ethiopia.**" And Herodotus said, **"There are two great Ethiopian nations, one in Sind (India) and the other in Egypt."**
> Recorded by Diodorus (Greek historian 100 B.C.)

Dialogue:
> Lycinus (describing an Egyptian): **'this boy is not merely black; he has thick lips** and his legs are too thin...his hair worn in a plait shows that he is not a freeman.'
> Timolaus: **'but that is a sign of really distinguished birth in Egypt,** Lycinus. All freeborn children plait their hair until they reach manhood...' (Lucian, _Navigations_, paras 2-3)

Dialogue:

Healing the Criminal Heart

Danaos (describing the Aegyptians (Egyptians)): 'I can see the crew with their **black limbs** and white tunics.' (Aeschylus, _The Suppliants_, vv. 719-20, 745)

The Egyptians were **"very black"** and the Ethiopians **'wooly haired."**

(See Aristotle, Physiognomy, Chap. VI).

Ancient Egyptian Depictions of Egyptians and Nubians

The Ancient Egyptians and Their Neighbors

From the Tomb of Ramses III: The four branches of mankind, according to the Egyptians: A- Egyptian as seen by himself, B- Indo-European, C- Other Africans, D- Semites (Middle Easterners). (Discovered by Cheikh Anta Diop)

Ancient Nubian/Egyptian man.

The images above clearly show that the Ancient Egyptian and the Nubians looked alike. One reason for the confusion about the ethnicity of the Ancient Egyptians is the misunderstanding about their depictions of themselves. There are three distinct forms, the red or reddish-brown, the brown and the black. Both of these are used interchangeably and this is what the early Egyptologists such as Champollion witnessed before the colors on many depictions had been damaged or lost. However, there are several images that have survived and from these it is possible to clearly see that the Ancient Egyptians depicted themselves with colors that were the same as those used to illustrate the Nubians. The pictures below are only one example. In any case, the depictions that have survived are supported by the statements of the ancient Greek writers themselves as well as the testimony and drawings of the European explorers of the early nineteenth century, who first uncovered the monuments and tomb inscriptions that were covered in sand, which had preserved the images up to that time but many of which have suffered due to vandalism by Arab/Muslim zealots, tourism, pollution ever since.

The images above from the tomb of Rameses III shows an Ancient Egyptian rendition of another man from the Sudan (Kush – Ethiopia). It is clear to see that the Egyptian peoples were originally of African descent and later mixed with the peoples from the neighboring lands and became a multicultural country.

The renowned Africologist Basil Davidson presented Dr. Diop briefly in Davidson's documentary program "Africa" and commented on this ancient ethnography and remarked that it was "rare," thus dismissing it as an anomaly. However, the following picture was discovered by Dr. Muata Ashby in the book _Arts and Crafts of Ancient Egypt_ by Flinders Petrie but not ascribed as an ethnography including Ancient Egyptians, but rather unknown "Abyssinians."

Ancient Egyptian Depiction of Ethnic Groups (New Kingdom Dynastic Period) (_Arts and Crafts of Ancient Egypt_, Flinders Petrie)

Healing the Criminal Heart

The picture above is an Ancient Egyptian depiction of the four ethnic groups of the ancient world. Described by Petrie as "the Four Races" the picture is one of the rare ethnographies that have come down to us from Ancient Egypt. To the far left is the face of a "Negro" (native African man). The next, from left to right, is a "Syrian" man, the third is described as an "Abyssinian" and the last is a "Libyan." Notice that there is supposed to be an Ancient Egyptian person in these class of art and having assigned the other "races" the Egyptian person has been omitted in the description of the group. This picture is a variation of the previous picture, discovered by Dr. Diop. If the picture is rendered as the original it would mean that the first man on the left that Petrie is refereeing to as a "Negro" is actually an Ancient Egyptian man. Since the practice of scarification is rare or unknown in Ancient Egypt the "Abyssinian" man would be the Nubian (Ethiopian) and the other person of African descent would have to be the Egyptian.

The term "Abyssinian" refers to languages often distinguished as belonging to the subgroup of Hamitic languages. The words Semitic (Asia Minor) and Hamitic (African) are derived from the names of Noah's sons, Shem and Ham (Christian Bible-Gen. 10). Ethiopia, formerly Abyssinia, is a republic in eastern Africa, currently bounded on the northeast by Eritrea and Djibouti, on the east and southeast by Somalia, on the southwest by Kenya, and on the west and northwest by Sudan. In ancient times the country was bounded in the north by Ancient Egypt. In ancient times Ethiopia and Egypt were strongly related. In fact, Ethiopia was the birthplace of the early Egyptians and also, according to Herodotus, the Indians as well. They appeared the same to him at the time of his travels through those countries. Thus, the picture shows that the Ancient Egyptians looked no different from other Africans.

"And upon his return to Greece, they gathered around and asked, "tell us about this great land of the Blacks called Ethiopia." And Herodotus said, "There are two great Ethiopian nations, one in Sind (India) and the other in Egypt."
—Herodotus (c. 484-425 BC)

Jean Fransçois Champollion (1790-1832), the main deciphered of the hieroglyphic text in the early 19th century remarked at the art he saw, which at the time was fully colored since the tombs and many other structures had been closed since the middle ages. He described images of the Ancient Egyptians created by them in which they made themselves look like the Ethiopians and concluded that they were of the same "race" as the modern day Nubians. It is unfortunate that due to the mishandling of the monuments due to the push for tourism, destruction and neglect by the Arab peoples and the harsh elements, many of the images that he saw cannot be seen today in their original form except for a limited amount of originals, like the one discovered by Dr. Diop or drawings made by people in his and other expeditions to Egypt. However, we have sufficient images and corroborating texts to say with certainty that the ethnicity of the original peoples who created the culture and civilization of the Nile Valley (Ancient Egypt) were the same in appearance as those people living in modern day Nubia, i.e. they were indeed "black" Africans.

One reason for the confusion about the ethnicity of the Ancient Egyptians is the misunderstanding about their depictions of themselves. There are two distinct forms, the red or reddish-brown and the black. Both of these are used interchangeably and this is what the early Egyptologists such as Champollion witnessed before the colors on many depictions had been damaged or lost.

Ancient Kamitan Terms and Ancient Greek Terms

In keeping with the spirit of the culture of Kamitan Spirituality, in this volume we will use the Kamitan names for the divinities through which we will bring forth the Philosophy of the Prt M Hru. Therefore, the Greek name Osiris will be converted back to the Kamitan (Ancient Egyptian) Asar (Ausar), the Greek Isis to Aset (Auset), the Greek Nephthys to Nebthet, Anpu to Anpu or Apuat, Hathor to Hetheru, Thoth or Hermes to Djehuti, etc. (see the table below) Further, the term Ancient Egypt will be used interchangeably with "Kemit" ("Kamit"), or "Ta-Meri," as these are the terms used by the Ancient Egyptians to refer to their land and culture.

Ancient Kamitan Terms and Ancient Greek Terms

Kamitan (Ancient Egyptian) Names	Greek Names
Amun	Zeus
Ra	Helios
Ptah	Hephastos
Nut	Rhea
Geb	Kronos
Net	Athena
Khonsu	Heracles
Set	Ares or Typhon
Bast	Artemis
Uadjit	Leto
Asar (Ausar)	Osiris or Hades
Aset (Auset)	Isis or Demeter
Nebthet	Nephthys
Anpu or Apuat	Anubis
Hetheru	Hathor (Aphrodite)
Heru	Horus or Apollo
Djehuti	Thoth or Hermes
Maat	Astraea or Themis

PART 1: Maat Philosophy Yoga and Mystical Religion

What are Yoga Philosophy and Ancient Egyptian Mystical Spirituality and What Significance does it hold for every human being?

This book is about Maat Philosophy. Maat Philosophy is the first stage of Shetaut Neter. Shetaut Neter means *"The Way of the Hidden Divinity."* This is what the Ancient Egyptians (Africans) called their religion. Maat Philosophy is also a discipline of Yoga. All of this will be introduced to you as you read this text and at the end you will be directed to how to practice these teachings to improve your life and what other books and materials you will need in order to practice these teachings effectively.

Most people think of spirituality and of God in terms of sectarian forms traditionally passed on by religious organizations. The Supreme Divinity is often seen as a powerful yet fearsome being who sends people to eternal damnation. However, in the light of Yoga philosophy and through the various disciplines developed by the yogic masters over the last 7,000 years, the Supreme Divinity is to be understood in a much more universal way. We not only discover the infinite compassion and love of the Self (Supreme Divinity) but through the various practices of Yoga, which have been tailored for the various levels of human spiritual development and different personalities, it is also possible to partake in the glory of Divinity. This is the goal of Yoga.

No matter how low a human being goes in his/her existence, the practice of Yoga with the correct understanding supplies a sure way to overcome any and all human ills, frailties and failings. This is true because all individuals are essentially one with the Divine Self. Through a process of ignorance they have forgotten their true identity. Through the process of Yoga, you may discover your true essence, thereby unleashing the gifts and infinite power of the soul.

With this inner power which comes from wisdom and self effort toward cleansing the heart from its negative emotions, feelings and thoughts, anyone can overcome incredible obstacles. This is the power that made it possible for the Ancient Egyptians to create the massive pyramids and temples out of stone without machinery. They were able to accomplish feats of engineering which modern society cannot duplicate. Even more importantly, they developed a science of spiritual development which has influenced all world religions and in the Egyptian Yoga Book Series, we show how the Ancient Egyptian elements are still present in Christianity, Islam, Hinduism, Buddhism and Taoism.

Healing the Criminal Heart

The heart of this science of self improvement is known to the world as *Yoga*. In recent times Yoga has been made popular by the Indian practitioners. In our book series we have shown that Indian Yoga is a continuation of the same teaching which was given in Ancient Egypt and that in ancient times Africa (where Egypt is located) was culturally connected to India. Many people have been introduced to yoga as a practice of physical exercise for health and relaxation, but in reality, Yoga is much more than that. Physical health and relaxation are only the beginning stage of yoga which is necessary in order to make it possible for a practitioner to understand and practice the higher teachings of self-development. Yoga is a vast science of self development which has proven its effectiveness over the last 7,000 years.

Many people, however, are interested in yoga philosophy from the ancient point of view. This is the perspective which we take in all of our books and literature. While we relate the teachings and show how other religions are all in reality aiming for the same goal, the upliftment of every human being, many people prefer the Ancient Egyptian myths, symbols, and practices.

We get many inquiries from inmates from all over the country. Usually when we are contacted by someone it is because they are searching for answers to long held spiritual questions. Life has not produced happy circumstances and there is an interest in anything that will alleviate the miseries and sorrows of life. They are looking for a way out. Our goal is to teach the ancient wisdom of true happiness and prosperity which has remained dormant or become distorted in the teachings of common religion. These inner teachings and practices can be followed by anyone who possesses maturity, sincerity and an honest desire to work toward self improvement.

Happiness can be yours on the condition that you are willing to work for it by practicing the art of self development. It does not matter what crime or what sin you have committed. The light of wisdom and the practices of purification can bring about a transformation in the consciousness of any human being. From the lower self you can move up to the Higher Self. This science begins with your understanding and forgiveness of yourself and then the intensive process of introspection and realization of the truth through building a life based on order, truth and justice.

Misery in life stems from the ignorance of one's true nature. Human beings are like a kings or queens who wander around the countryside as beggars, not knowing their true identity. They act as a beggars, treat others unkindly, indulge in hatred and anger of others, they are frustrated due to their condition and don't know what to do about it so they go on from day to day wasting their lives. You are unaware of your talents and of your capacity to love yourself and others. You have come to a state which has led you to experience the degradation and loss of spiritual and physical freedom. You search for excitement and fulfillment of your desires through your worldly relationships, by entertaining yourself with the media, drugs or alcohol, or by acquiring objects (cars, clothes, etc.) that you think will make you happy. You do these things because you have been taught that this is the way to pursue happiness. But have any of these things brought you true and lasting happiness and peace? In order to be truly happy you must unleash your spirit. You are the one responsible for your condition because of your past actions based on ignorance. Therefore, do not

Healing the Criminal Heart

waste any more time by blaming others or by seeking to find explanations in society or other external causes. The wonderful thing is that you are also the one who by your actions illumined by the light of wisdom in action (Maat), can change your life.

The Ancient Egyptians prescribed one solution to all of the problems of life and they built an entire country based on this precept and the legacy lives on up to this day. The solution is *Know Thyself.* Through self knowledge, all of the misconceptions of the mind which have led to degraded states, erroneous thoughts, conflict and misunderstanding are washed away. Through self knowledge one discovers the supreme happiness which comes from inner contentment and peace which cannot come from external objects or relationships in the world.

Your interest (reading this volume) indicates that you have begun to recognize that there is a higher goal in life for you other than your current experience. This is a blessing because most people are not able to see the misery of their own condition and then to do something about it. Most people are caught in the web of negativity they have woven in their minds and go on like robots from one miserable situation to another. Your task is to follow up on this contact, study the teachings and begin practicing them in your life right now. Develop a relationship with your inner Higher Self and discover the strength to overcome your failings. Everyone is a child of the Divine, as such everyone is capable of supreme good according to their level of awareness of their true self.

There is no fanatical or magical way to self development except to learn the science of self knowledge and to then apply the teachings and practice the exercises for spiritual development by gradually incorporating them into your life. You will have many ups and downs when you begin to practice. Sometimes you will not be able to follow the teachings because you are overcome by your established negative ways. But if your sincerely press on, in time you will discover the source of inner strength within you. Self development is an inner attainment, it is revealed in your level of peace and oneness with the universe, your level of joy and love for humanity; not in the level of callousness or egoistic selfishness or apathy toward others or the possessions you seem to own or the status accorded by others. Many people confuse apathy or uncaring toward others as peace but this is an intense form of selfishness and hard-heartedness which masquerades as peace but is in reality a form of unrest and inner pain which reaches to the very soul.

What is a convict? The dictionary defines "convict" as a person found guilty of a crime, especially one serving a prison sentence. Is this guilt or prison sentence a part of your eternal existence? Is it a permanent blot on your soul which will send you to hell for ever? The wisdom of yoga has taught for thousands of years that the soul is innately divine and has a possibility to evolve, to discover its own higher reality which is eternal and pure in the Supreme Self (God). This means that it is possible to overcome and transcend any and all forms of negativity or evil actions of the past. This exalted vision of life is not merely a myth inspired by superstition or fanaticism but is was the basis of Ancient Egyptian society which allowed the construction of the most extensive and longest running civilization in history. Ancient Egyptian dynastic civilization existed for over 5,000 years. No other civilization in history can compare to this record. What made the Ancient Egyptians great? It was the spiritual basis of society which was rooted in *Shetaut Neter* (spiritual values) and *Maat* (virtue).

A person may be ordered to be obedient, to follow rules, etc. However, if the ten commandments and so many other laws are established in society why then is it that there is increasing crime and increasing strife among people? Why is there enmity in the world? Why is there a desire to hurt others? Why is there a desire to misappropriate the property of others?

Anger and hatred cannot be stopped by simply telling someone to be good, loving, forgiving and so on. One cannot become righteous by being ordered to or forced to, no more than a plant can be forced to grow, bear fruit or flowers through a command by the farmer. One can be compelled to follow rules but this does not mean that one is necessarily a virtuous person. Many people do not commit crimes and yet they are not virtuous because they are harboring negative thoughts (violence, hatred, greed, lust, etc.) in their hearts. Virtue is a profound quality which every human being has a potential to manifest because it is the innate nature of the innermost reality within every human being. This is because the innermost self of every person is divine. However, the revelation of this truth requires effort on the part of the individual as well as the correct guidance. Virtue is like a flower which can grow and become beautiful for the whole world to see. However, just as a plant must receive the proper nutrients (soil, water, sunlight, etc.) so too the human heart must receive the proper caring and nurturing in the form of love, wisdom, proper diet, meditation and good will.

What is Virtue and How can it Transform the Heart?

In ancient Egypt the name for virtue was *Maat*. But who or what is Maat? The ancient Egyptian creation story states that when Ra (Supreme Being) emerged in his barque out of the primeval waters for the first time when he brought creation into being, he was standing on the pedestal of Maat. Thus the Creator, Ra, lives by Maat and has established Creation on Maat. Who is Maat? Maat represents the very order which maintains creation. Therefore, it is said that Ra created the universe by putting Maat in the place of chaos. So creation itself is Maat. Creation without order is chaos. Maat is a profound teaching in reference to the nature of creation and the manner in which human conduct should be cultivated. It refers to a deep understanding of Divinity and the manner in which virtuous qualities can be developed in the human heart so as to come closer to the Divine.

> *"Those who live today will die tomorrow, those who die tomorrow will be born again; Those who live MAAT will not die."*
> -Ancient Egyptian Proverb

Maat is a philosophy, a spiritual symbol as well as a cosmic energy or force which pervades the entire universe. She is the symbolic embodiment of world order, justice, righteousness, correctness, harmony and peace. She is also known by her headdress composed of a feather of truth. She is a form of the Goddess Aset, who represents wisdom and spiritual awakening through balance and equanimity.

Healing the Criminal Heart

Virtue is the path of righteousness, peace and inner expansion of the heart. It is latent in every human heart but needs to be awakened and developed in order for its benefits to be reaped. In modern society the ten commandments are known about but they are simply memorized and then forgotten, never to be practiced or studied. The teachings of the Asarian Resurrection Myth of Ancient Egypt and the precepts of Maat are a profound teaching in reference to the human heart and how the negative tendencies can cloud the intellect and cause a human being to become even lower than and animal. In the pursuit of happiness or what people have come to feel will bring happiness, the most heinous atrocities have been committed throughout history and these same acts of unrighteousness have led to the destruction of the perpetrator. So why does vice and unrighteousness continue to exist in the world?

The Forms of Maat

All souls come to the earth for the purpose of discovering true happiness. They are in search for true fulfillment, true contentment. However, this desire becomes degraded when the soul of a human being sinks into ignorance about where that happiness can be found. This condition leads to negative experiences, negative thoughts and negative feelings, which produce more negativity. The soul finds itself in a sea of negativity. When there is no higher vision of life, despair, restlessness, passion, greed, anger, violence and desire rule the heart and cloud the intellect. The person does not think about the consequences nor the correctness or wrongness of their actions. It then becomes possible to lie, cheat and steal, all in an effort to gain what they think they want, what they believe will satisfy their need. They become capable of hurting others and susceptible to being hurt by others, manipulated by others and ultimately they lead themselves to experiences of pain and sorrow such as failed relationships, trouble with the law, inability to experience mental peace, disappointments, frustrations, illness, etc.

Adversity in Life

Why is there adversity in life? Wouldn't it be nice if there was no misfortune or unluckiness to hamper your movement in life? Shouldn't God have created a perfect world? Human life abounds with adversity. Even the very rich experience adversity. In fact, no matter who you are you will experience adversity of one form or another as you progress through life. This is an expression of cosmic justice.

40

Healing the Criminal Heart

Adversity is a divine messenger. Imagine how life would be if you could do anything you wanted to do. You would indulge every desire and whim. You would only seek to satisfy your desire for pleasure and you would not accomplish any thing significant in life. In the end you would be frustrated and disappointed because no matter how hard you try it is not possible to ever completely satisfy your desire for the pleasures of the senses.

Adversity is a form of resistance which life places on all beings for the purpose of engendering in them a need to strive to overcome the desires of the lower nature and thus to discover the Higher Self within. When adversity is met with the correct understanding and with the right attitude it can become a great source of strength and spiritual inspiration. However, if adversity makes you hardhearted, insensitive, selfish, cold and bitter then you will lead yourself deeper into the quagmire of negativity and pain. Adversity is God's way of calling your attention away from negative ways of life and to draw attention toward the basic elements of life. Often when people succeed in acquiring some object they desired they develop conceit and vanity. They look down on others and feel proud of their accomplishment, not realizing that their achievement will fulfill them only temporarily. However, when they lose what they desired they fall into the valley of adversity and to despair, violence and anger. They blame others for their misfortune and seek to hurt others for their loss.

Many of those people who have experienced the most adversity in history include Sages and Saints. Why should God allow those who are trying to be closest to the Divine be plagued with adversity? The answer lies in an Ancient Egyptian proverb:

> "Adversity is the seed of well doing; it is the nurse of heroism and boldness; who that hath enough, will endanger himself to have more? Who that is at ease, will set their life on the hazard?

Have you noticed that it seems as though the people who are most righteous and deserving of prosperity are the one's who suffer the most in life? In families, the child who is most obedient gets the most attention and disciplinary control. People who were loving and compassionate suffer illnesses and pain from others. This is because nature has been set up by God to create situations which challenge human beings so as to provide for them opportunities to discover their inner resources which give them the capacity to overcome the trouble and thereby grow in discovery of their deeper self. Those who suffer most are in reality those who have drawn more attention from the Divine, indeed they are chosen for more intense spiritual testing and training. This testing process of nature allows every soul the opportunity to face trouble with either boldness and faith or with fear and negativity. The rewards of adversity faced well are increased strength of will and an increased feeling of discovery of the Divine within (inner peace and expansion -Heaven). When adversity is faced with negativity and ignorance it leads to pain, sorrow and more adversity (Hell).

Healing the Criminal Heart

Therefore, adversity cannot be understood and successfully faced with negativity (anger, hatred, hard-heartedness, etc.). Adversity can only be overcome with wisdom and virtue and virtue is the first and most important quality to be developed by all serious spiritual aspirants.

From a spiritual point of view what is considered to be prosperity by the masses of ignorant people is in reality adversity and what is considered to be adversity by the masses is in reality prosperity. The masses consider that becoming rich and being able to indulge the pleasures of the senses through food, drink, drugs and sex is the ultimate goal, yet is there anyone who has discovered true peace and contentment even with billions of dollars? Having the opportunity to indulge the pleasures of the senses creates an opportunity for the mind to become more dependent on the worldly pleasures. This process intensifies the egoistic feelings and draws the soul away from discovering *Hetep* (true peace) within. There is increasing agitation and worry over gaining what is desired and then preoccupation with how to hold onto it. Not realizing that all must be left behind at the time of death anyway. People keep on seeking worldly fame, fortune and glory and in the process never discover true happiness and peace. They have duped themselves into believing that material wealth brings happiness because the greedy corporations, the media and popular culture reinforce this message. In reality it is a philosophy of ignorance based on lack of reflection and spiritual insight. Adversity is a call to wake up from this delusion of pain and sorrow and those who are experiencing the worst conditions are receiving the loudest call. Therefore, adversity is in reality prosperity because it stimulates the mind through suffering so that it may look for a higher vision of life and discover the abode of true happiness, peace and contentment which transcends all worldly measures.

This exalted vision of life is the innate potential of every human being. What is necessary is the dedication and perseverance to seek a higher understanding of the divine nature of creation and the divine nature of the innermost heart. Your inner Higher Self has the power to absolve and redeem all negativity. This is the highest goal of all human beings and the most difficult one as well. However, as you gain greater understanding and greater will to act with virtue your vision of the divine will increase and draw you closer and closer to the Higher Self. This is the glory of virtue and its power to vanquish and eradicate vice from the human heart.

"Kmn" – ignorance

"There is no darkness like the darkness of Ignorance."
-Ancient Egyptian Proverb

What is Virtue?

Virtue is the quality which implies harmony with the universe. Virtue is that which leads a human being to come into harmony with the Divine (God). From a mythological standpoint, sin is to be understood as the absence of wisdom which leads to righteousness, harmony and peace and the existence of ignorance which leads to mental unrest, conflict and the endless desires of the mind. Sin operates in human life as any movement which works against self-discovery, and virtue is any movement toward discovering the essential truth of the innermost heart. The state of ignorance will end only when the mind develops a higher vision. It must look beyond the illusions of human desire and begin to seek something more substantial and abiding. This is when the aspirant develops an interest in spirituality and the practice of order, correctness, self-improvement, purification and intellectual development. These qualities are symbolized by MAAT and Apuat-Anpu (Anubis) is the symbol of the discerning intellect which can see right from wrong, good from evil, truth from untruth, etc.

The God Anpu

Where Does Sin and Negativity Come From?

When a child is born does that child know anything about the associations and acquaintances he or she will make? Do they know about the either the good or bad people they will meet? Do they know about the negative things they will do in the future? There are many factors which determine the actions which an individual will perform in their lifetime. The most important of these is the tendency that person carried forth from the previous lifetimes. You are not a finite, mortal human being. In reality you are an eternal soul, wandering in the realm of physical nature as you take birth again and again (reincarnation) in search of true happiness and peace. Your search has led you to thousands of past lives wherein you experienced prosperity and adversity as well as degrees of sinfulness and virtue. If there was a tendency to negative thoughts in the past lifetime there may be a tendency for more negativity in this lifetime if it is stimulated and not opposed. (see *Meditation: The Ancient Egyptian path to Enlightenment* by Dr. Muata Ashby)

Fig A. The God Set

The most important thing to remember now is that your present effort can overcome any and all of your past negativity if you apply yourself with earnestness and resolve to become fully established in virtue. This means that you must decide to dedicate your life to discovering and facing all shades of vice and negativity within you and in so doing never fall back into the pits of ignorance which lead to pain and sorrow.

Having forgotten your eternal nature you have been wandering through many lifetimes, meeting many other souls in the form of friends, relatives, etc. who are also wandering travelers, also seeking the same thing as you are: peace and contentment. However, when the soul forgets its eternal, loving and virtuous nature it becomes indoctrinated by society and takes on the values and beliefs of society. If society says that money is most important then the masses of ignorant people do whatever they can to get money. Those who cannot do it legally do it by any other means because they have lost the connection to their fellow souls due to the delusion of ignorance caused by the pressure of desires and mental agitation. If those around them call them bad they begin to think "I am a bad person" and then proceed to think of themselves as evil and unconsciously they generate thoughts of anger, hatred, envy, etc. which cause them untold miseries though many lifetimes. The universe is one connected essence. When you allow negativity in your mind you are communing with the negative thoughts from all over the universe. This is why it is important, especially in the beginning of your yogic practices, to break with all negative associations to as well as with negative habits (drugs, Tabasco, vices, rudeness, cursing, worldly people, etc.) to the extent that is possible while keeping company with those who are wise, virtuous, loving and peaceful.

In reality, there is no real "badness" in the true you, the deepest part of you. Your soul is in reality pure and full of love which is waiting to be discovered. However, your ego is like a blanket of dust which has settles on a piece of glass and obstructs the light from passing through. When you live according to the precepts of virtue, the dust of ignorance, shame, desire, hatred, anger, lust, envy, greed, etc. are removed from your being and then it is possible for you to discover the treasure which lies within your own heart. When this treasure arises in the heart it has an effect on others. This is the source of divine qualities (forgiveness, love, peace, harmony, charity, sharing, kindness, etc.) which a spiritual aspirant can share with the world. Thus, there is in reality no such thing as a criminal heart, only hearts which are clamoring for freedom from the bonds of ignorance and fear.

Fig. B The God Heru

45

In the Ancient Egyptian Myth of Asar there is a teaching in reference to the god named Set (Fig A). Set is the embodiment of evil, greed, lust, hatred envy, etc. He killed his own brother (Asar) to steal his Kingdom (Egypt). Heru (Fig. B), Asar' son confronts Set and a battle ensues. Heru eventually overcomes Set through virtue. Set is redeemed and transformed into a positive force for good. However, at the end it is revealed that Heru and Set are in reality not two personalities (Fig. C) but indeed one and the same. So the idea behind the teaching is that the true enemy is not outside of you but within your very own personality and it exists there in the form of negative qualities which in effect fetter your higher vision of spiritual reality. They cloud your intellect and deteriorate the willpower so they allow sinfulness and unrighteousness. However, the love, sweetness and wisdom of the divine is also there within you and this divine essence is equipped with immense spiritual force which can be discovered and used for developing a positive vision which can eradicate all negativity and reveal the true you as the sun is revealed when the clouds disperse after a storm.

Fig. C Heru-Set

Where Does True Happiness Come From?

In reality, happiness does not and cannot come from objects that can be acquired or from activities that are performed or from people outside of yourself. It can only come from within. Even actions that seem to be pleasurable in life cannot be considered as a source of happiness from a philosophical point of view because all activities are relative. This means that one activity is pleasurable for one person and painful for another. Also, all forms of physical pleasure are fleeting. They do not fulfill the mind for long. This leads to the realization that it is not the activity itself that holds the happiness but the individual doer who is performing the action and assigning a value to it which she or he has learned from society to assign. Therefore, if it was learned that going out to a party is supposed to be fun then that activity will be pursued as a source of happiness. Here action is performed in pursuit of the fruit of the action in the form happiness; a result is desired from the action. However, there are several negative psychological factors which arise that will not allow true happiness to manifest. The first is that the relentless pursuit of the action renders the mind restless and agitated. This prevents inner peace from entering the mind. The second is that if the desired activity is not possible there will be depression in the mind. If the activity is thwarted by some outside force, meaning that something or someone prevented you from achieving the object or activity you saw as the "source of happiness" you develop anger toward that person or circumstance. If by chance you succeed in achieving the object or activity you become elated and this will cause greed in the mind, you will want more and more of it. When you are not able to get more at any particular time you will become depressed and disappointed. Therefore, under these conditions a constant dependence on outside activities and worldly objects develops in the mind which will not allow for true peace and contentment. Even though it is illogical to pursue activities which cause pain in life people are constantly acting against their own interests as they engage in actions in an effort to gain happiness while in reality they are enhancing the probability of encountering pain later on. People often act and shortly regret what they have done. Sometimes people know even at the time of their actions that they are wrong and yet they are unable to stop themselves. This is because when the mind is controlled by desires and expectations the intellect, the light of reason, and will power are *clouded* and *dull*. However, when the mind is controlled by the intellect, then it is not possible to be led astray due to the *fantasies* and *illusions* of the mind which engender irrational desires. When the individual is guided by their intellect, then only right actions can be performed no matter what negative ideas arise in the mind. Such a person can not be deluded into negative actions and when negative actions (actions which lead to future pain and disappointments) are not performed then unhappiness cannot exist. Thus, a person who lives according to the teachings of RIGHTEOUS ACTION lives a life of perpetual peace and happiness in the present. This implies performing actions without desire or expectations for the future results of those actions and expecting only to do good to humanity in service of Maat (God).

Thus, true peace and inner fulfillment will never come through pursuit of actions when there is an expectation or desire for the fruits of those actions based on egoistic notions and ignorance. The belief in objects or worldly activities as a source of happiness if therefore seen as a state known as *spiritual ignorance* wherein the individual is caught up in the illusions, fantasies and fanciful notions of the mind. However, happiness and peace can arise spontaneously when there is an attitude of detachment and dispassion toward objects and situations in life and attachment to what is good, beautiful and true. If actions are performed with the idea of discovering peace within, based on the understanding of the philosophy outlined above, and for the sake of the betterment of society, then these actions will have the effect of purifying the heart of the individual. The negative desires and expectations will dwindle while the inner fulfillment and awareness of fulfillment in the present moment will increase. There will be greater and greater discovery of peace within; a discovery of what is truly stable and changeless within as opposed to the mind and outer world which are constantly changing and unpredictable.

The Role of Sexuality in Human Relationships and Society

Modern society and mass culture promote sexuality as a means to feel good about oneself. As an eternality, sexuality as all other aspects of human life, cannot be depended on just as one cannot depend on the weather. The Self within (Maat) is the only abiding reality which can be counted upon in life. Therefore, on a very basic logical level, the dependence on sexuality as a means to feel wanted, youthful or vital is in reality a profound farce into which the human mind has fallen. As old age sets in those who have based their life on the dependence on sex and the fulfillment of egoistic desires begin to feel lost because they cannot keep up the activities of the past. This is the source of mid life crisis as well as adultery, sexual violence and many other problems in relationships.

Relationships which are based on sex, demands, and expectations are doomed to experience strife because none of these are stable factors even in ordinary relationships which do not include sexual intercourse (friends, co-workers, family relations, etc.). The source of the problem lies in the ignorance of the higher purpose and destiny of the human soul. Sexual energy is the driving force of life and its purpose is to assist the soul in carrying out the goals of a lifetime, specifically to gain knowledge and wisdom of the Self which leads to enlightenment (see *Egyptian Tantra Yoga* by Dr. Muata Ashby). This is accomplished through promoting a process which leads to the development and integration of the intellectual and emotional elements of one's psyche through the relationships, occupation and life situations. If the relationships, occupation and life situations have as the main goal to provide pleasure, then they are doomed to failure. However, if they are based on the understanding that they are tools which the soul has been given to promote spiritual advancement they can be as a ladder to heaven.

So relationships based on spiritual principles should not be demanding or promoting expectations from others. Many people develop the idea that if a partner does not want to engage in sex that this means the partner is losing love or having an adulterous affair. Under these circumstances there is no trust in the relationship because "love" has been equated with sex, something which is fleeting and superficial. This ignorant understanding leads to the belief that the absence of sex and passion means an absence of love and pleasure. Often times the feeling of being wanted and appreciated has been equated with love and so people seek sexual relations or sentimental shows of attachment as a means to feel wanted and appreciated. Many people set conditions for their love and impose demands on others: "If you do this I will do that for you", "If you don't do this then that means that you don't love me," etc. These statements are based on ignorance, immaturity and dependence and will inevitably lead to strife, disappointment and unrest.

A true relationship will not be based on sexuality, demands or conditions. Many times people have children as a means to feel manly or motherly, or as a means to trap a partner or as a means to bring someone into the world whom they can love and love them back, not thinking of the consequences or the illusoriness of their own logic. However, through understanding, forgiveness, control of the sexual urge and the development of higher goals in life, sex, progeny and virtuous vows can be a means to discover a greater connection in a relationship. True love and friendship are like an open door. There will be no conditions or demands even though there may be disagreements or the need to chastise a friend for wrong doing. When a relationship is based on these principles each partner can feel secure and not need to search for understanding or comfort elsewhere. As old age sets in, both have set into motion a process wherein the sexual feelings have been sublimated into a spiritual union with each other as well as with the higher Self within that transcends any form of physical contact. When life is based on selfishness, personal desires, demands and fear it leads to sorrow and contraction in consciousness leading to intensification of egoism and all of the negative qualities in human nature. When life is lived based on the principles of mystical spirituality it leads to expansion in consciousness and the unfoldment of universal love in the human heart. Therefore, peace and harmony are promoted and enhanced as life goes on. While true love is universal, this should not be taken to mean that the mystical teachings promote a philosophy commonly referred to as "free love". In reality, the modern free love movement which promotes promiscuity and multiple partners is an escape from the true necessity of life which is sexual restraint. It is an attempt to justify and promote increased sexual activity with multiple partners in an attempt to achieve greater sexual gratification. In the end this movement leads to depletion of the vital forces and will power and it promotes mental unrest and disappointment in relationships as well as the inability to discover true love and caring. Universal love, from the mystical point of view, implies discovering that all life is an expression of the Divine and that one's very self, the innermost reality within the heart, is filled with boundless love and peace for all. Therefore universal love refers to a caring that encompasses the entire universe. It is a vision which comes from living a life of selflessness and public service. When these principles are promoted, the desire for expressing sexual feelings gives way to the higher purposes of life. When this occurs, great inventions and advancements in all areas of society are brought forth from the men and women who are able to control, sublimate and transcend the gross level of sexual expression. In this context, those who act for the benefit of others, those who work for the benefit of humanity, those who promote peace and harmony in society as parents promote peace and harmony in a family are to be considered as advanced souls. Their legacy is the light of knowledge, peace, harmony, virtue and love which inspire others to achieve great heights in life. Universal love is the promotion of universal peace and justice for all. It implies sharing one's skills and expertise for the purpose of lifting others up so that they may experience the elevated levels of human existence and spiritual glory. It implies an understanding that even those who do evil deeds have the same divine basis which is only misguided due to ignorance. Therefore, universal love implies forgiveness and the willingness to chastise others when they commit evil acts in order that they should learn the proper way to live. Universal love is a most advanced and powerful development in human evolution and at its heights it leads to universal consciousness and spiritual enlightenment, in effect, communing with the universal source of love, the Supreme Self (God) which is referred to as resurrection and immortality.

> "When opulence and extravagance are a necessity instead of righteousness and truth, society will be governed by greed and injustice."
>
> -Ancient Egyptian Proverb

Healing the Criminal Heart

When society bases its values on sex and material wealth, there develops a process wherein young people become misguided as to the purpose of life and set out to satisfy the urges of the lower self as soon as possible. Oblivious to the higher spiritual reality, young people confuse love with sex, money and fame and thus travel the self destructive path wherein their actions lead to detrimental situations and the decay of society. An example of this is the growing numbers of teen-age mothers who desired to become pregnant in order to "have somebody to love" and or to "get a boy to love and stay with them". The boys on the other hand feel that "sex is a pleasure tool and that if the girl got pregnant it is her problem", and so they shirk any responsibility. Others feel that females are objects to be used and so treat them as possessions to be controlled against their will. Others profess to be devoid of sexual misconduct simply because they do not say or do things which are considered evil by society. However, in their thoughts they harbor desires, longings and other secret expectations and these inevitable lead to gross expressions in the form of disapproval of others, hatred, lust, resentment, etc. against others. Further, those who do not speak out against evil under the misguided notion that non-violence means no conflict are also part of the negativity. Speaking out is an expression of spiritual strength and wisdom which do not require violence and negativity. Emotionalism and animosity are hindrances to good speech. Speaking is an art to be performed when it will do the most good and not for idle talk or for showing off to others or to those who do not wish to listen. A person becomes weak when they are constantly chasing after the egoistic desires. Therefore, spiritual strength and will power to resist and fight against injustice and violence increases when there is self-control, inner peace and self-discovery.

Procreation is a tool of nature which it uses to bring about the possibility for spiritual evolution. When it is used for the purpose of personal pleasure it will lead to pain, sorrow and lack of fulfillment. However, if it is used as a part of life when a relationship is ready to produce offspring then it is a source of inspiration, greater closeness and spiritual awareness. An advanced society should not promote sexual intercourse before the age of 25 and outside of a situation wherein the parents will be responsible and be able to care for the child. Also the society should be ready to assist in caring for the child. Every member of society should be expected to promote justice and righteousness by chastising and educating any child wherever he or she may be acting in a negative way. This principle follows an ancient African tradition embodied in the proverb: "It takes a whole village to raise one child". Therefore, the society is also responsible for the development of children and it will be the recipient of the positive or negative development of every member of society. Thus, if society is overwhelmed due to the social problems promiscuity and population control should be promoted as an ideal until the problems are under control. The problems of societal institutions stem from the problems of individuals who are misguided by erroneous notions (egoistic desires and materialistic goals). Therefore, in order to alleviate the problems of society, the values by which families and individuals within the society live by must be virtuous and just (Maat).

All of the aberrant behaviors which have been outlined above, that are in contradiction with the precepts of MAAT (righteousness, truth) develop out of the ignorance of the true meaning and purpose of life. The soul uses the body in order to progress spiritually. In reality it is neither male nor female but chooses one of these in order to gain specific forms of knowledge and experience. In general, when the soul needs to develop in the area of emotions it incarnates as a female personality; when the need to develop in the area of reasoning is emphasized it incarnates as a male personality. However, through the process of reincarnation it has experienced many male and female lifetimes. Therefore, the egoism and vanity of maleness or femaleness, the pride, conceit and indulgence in sexuality, adornments of the body, preoccupation with attractiveness, in gross as well as subtle ways, is in reality an expression of ignorance of the truth of the soul.

The level of maturity in an individual may be gauged by the values which are held. If an individual values that which is transient, ephemeral and superficial this is clearly a sign of spiritual immaturity. If the values given more importance are those things which are lasting and abiding, and which lead to truth, wisdom and justice, then the individual is moving toward spiritual maturity and emancipation from the world of human pain and suffering. In the same way, societies may be measured as to their level of development. If a society promotes that which is superficial it is considered to be immature. In Ancient Egypt, the tallest and largest buildings were the temples. In fact, the largest structure, known to the ancient world is the temple known today as the Great Pyramid at Giza. This shows that Ancient Egyptian society placed spiritual values above those of the lower nature. In modern times, society placed the greatest value on sex, money, and fame. This is proven by the sky scrapers dedicated to commerce and finance. Spiritual wealth in the form of mental peace and self-discovery are abiding principles which are carried forth after death. Sex, money and fame are only useful when there is a body to experience these with and after death they cause unrest and anxiety for the soul. Therefore, the predilection (a disposition in favor of something; preference) toward the superficial, egoistic values of life denotes immaturity as a civilization and foreshadows future disharmony in society.

The predilection toward material values produces progeny who become the embodiment of Setian feelings, emotions and desires (anger, greed, unrest, egoism, selfishness, conceit, vanity, pleasure seeking, personal gratification, etc.) which lead to callousness, hard-heartedness and predatory behaviors towards others. With these feelings it becomes possible to desecrate all that is good even while professing to be righteous and upstanding, while insidiously engineering the destruction of others for personal gain. Examples of this are to be found not only in the ordinary criminal ranks of society who openly engage in violence, stealing and selling substances which promote physical and mental deterioration (poisons such as drugs, alcohol and tobacco) but also in society at large. Some examples include medical doctors who tell patients that they must have operations even when they don't need them, lawyers who promote litigation in order to gain more fees, business people who sell products which are not good for society (items which promote pollution, do not work as advertised, promote the prurient interests (pornography), promote vanity and self self-centeredness, etc.).

The sublimation of the sex drive is the mother of all sublime thoughts and aspirations in human consciousness as well as the source for the power (will) to carry those visions to completion. Thus, procreation as well as the creative expression of consciousness in the form of inventions and social advancements, both have their proper place in the scheme which has been set forth by the Divine, through the medium of nature and human evolution.

Conclusion to Part 1

When you learn to open your heart you will initially discover the negativity which has led you to untoward situations in your life, but just as a diamond is hidden in the encrusted, hardened piece of carbon, your luminous higher self is hidden behind your hardened ego and its selfishness. True spirituality means moving toward the Divine. Moving toward the Divine means leaving behind the pettiness and negativity of the ego. Egoism (chaos) cannot exist where there is righteousness, truth, order and justice (Maat). When you learn to cleanse yourself of this selfishness you will discover the true self within you. This is a new birth which does not occur from the union of a man and a woman or in a hospital or in a church. It occurs in your very heart. You can begin right now, wherever you are, to practice the ancient teachings. You can learn to use adversity as your teacher. Indeed your adversity has directed you to seek out spiritual counseling. Therefore, there is some good in adversity.

No jail can change a human being. Only you can cause a true transformation in your own life. In reality there are no criminal hearts but there are people who live life based on ignorance and negativity. Ignorance and negativity are the path of pain and sorrow in life and the life hereafter. When the ignorance and negativity are removed, then it is possible to have a real transformation of the heart. This kind of transformation is not like those people who simply change from one vice only to pick up another. This kind of transformation offers an opportunity to discover a greater world wherein the mistakes of the past become the tools for enlightenment as you begin to understand the reasons and causes of all events in your life. The science of the Yoga of Action (Maat Philosophy) is the gateway to positive human evolution through positive self-effort. As you become aware of your divine gifts you will be able to heal yourself and share and uplift others. It is recommend that you take up the study of the books *The Asarian Resurrection, The Wisdom of Maati, Initiation Into Egyptian Yoga* and *The Mind of Set.* These will help you to set up your own personal spiritual practice and will answer many questions about Maat Philosophy and the Character of Set in Ancient Egyptian psycho-mythology. Proper guidance is an essential part of correct spiritual development. We have attempted to provide a book series which will lead you to understanding. The rest is now up to you now.

Some final thoughts...

Many people believe they are free due to their many possessions or status. In reality they are slaves to their desires and this bondage causes them to experience the many problems of life. True spirituality is that science which leads to understanding, inner discovery and expansion in consciousness. When these occur in the human heart ignorance is eradicated and true freedom is achieved. This is true freedom and inner fulfillment which cannot be derived or affected by outer conditions or circumstances.

Those who desire to tread the path of Maat should allow their devotional feeling to flow toward the Divine mother, Maat. You must begin to feel that your actions, thoughts and words are those of the Goddess. Place yourself in her hands and allow her loving hand to guide you. Feel that the adversity you have created for yourself will be overcome through the grace of Maat. See adversity as lessons from the divine mother and chant her name in adoration and praise as the very source of your strength and will to destroy what is ignorant and sinful within yourself so as to purify your heart. You must engage yourself in selfless service. Even if you volunteer and do not receive payment, feel that you are rendering service to humanity in the name of the Goddess and feel that she is working through you to help others as she purifies your heart in the process. Eventually you will be lead, through a mystical process, toward an occupation which will be uplifting, fulfilling for you and beneficial to humanity. Along with this, practice meditation, prayer, study of the teachings and chanting as part of your spiritual disciplines. Chant thus:

"Om Maati am Maak-heru"
"Om Maati am Maak-heru"
(The Divine Self manifesting as Maati, grant that I become purified and enlightened)

May the grace of the Divine Mother be upon you.
Anyone who is seriously and sincerely interested in studying the path of Maat should begin by reading and applying the teachings presented in the book: *The Wisdom of Maati* by Dr. Muata Ashby. The Egyptian Yoga Book Series has been created for those who would like to explore the various paths of Yoga science from the Ancient Egyptian perspective. However, Maat is the foundation of all other paths because the practice of Maat purifies the heart and allows a person to become a vessel for higher spiritual realization. Therefore, a person who has experienced adversity in life must realize that they are the cause of their own misery but that through proper feeling, thinking and action they can rise above error, doubt and sinfulness (negativity).

PART II: How to Adopt the Path of Ancient Egyptian Spirituality

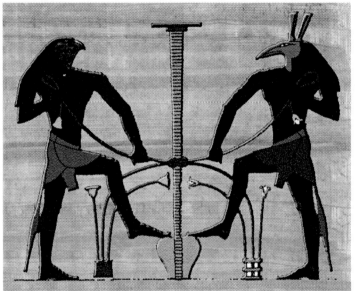

"Sema Heru-Set"

The image above is another rendition the concept of reuniting Heru and Set. The divinities representing Virtue (Heru) and Vice (Set) actually make peace and in so doing foment a "Sems" or union. In the same manner, the aspirant who wants to overcome the vices needs to engender a movement towards virtue. This allows the personality to be purified and then the true essential being emerges shining brightly to illuminate the individual and all who come into contact with him or her. Therefore, even the most impure being can transform into the highest Sage.

Hetep!

FOREWORD TO PART II

First of all I would like to thank all of you who have supported the reemergence of Ancient Egyptian Wisdom as we head towards the new millennium. It is good to see that so many people are rediscovering the teachings which lead to peace and blessedness.

This book is a continuation of *Healing The Criminal Heart: Introduction to Maat Philosophy (Part 1), Yoga and Spiritual Redemption Through the Path of Virtue*. This was a landmark work which applied the teachings of Ancient Egyptian Maat Philosophy to the problems of modern life and especially those of people who find themselves caught up in the cycle of criminal behavior and activities which lead to their destruction as well as the destruction of others.

This book series is not just for those who may find themselves incarcerated in a jail or penitentiary since there are many forms of bondage. There are many people who think that they are free because they can walk the streets and do whatever they want to do. This is of course a fallacy because nobody can do whatever they want to do. Everyone is subject to the constraints of something. Some are under the constraints of parents, others are under the constraints of other authorities, others feel they are under the constraints of a higher organization, etc. Ultimately all people are under the constraints of nature. You can't live for more than a few minutes without breathing or a few days without water or a few weeks without food. These are real constraints. However, there is one more major constraint that affects everyone: IGNORANCE.

Ignorance is the greatest cause of bondage for a human being and even animals are free of this constraint. This means that even animals enjoy life more than an ordinary human being! Animals do not worry so much that they loose sleep or feel guilt so as to feel miserable or become frustrated when they cannot get a television, car or jewelry. Yet people suffer over these things every day.

Of course there are real injustices in the world, racism, sexism, drug pushing, capitalism, exploitation of native societies, prostitution, the conspiracy to miseducate all people through a poorly equipped school system, the promotion of gun dealing, the promotion of meat eating, etc. But why is it that some people seem to rise above these scourges of society and discover an inner peace and strength which acts as a pillar for the community? What is it in them that allows them to get through the day and to avoid being caught in the system which is bent on controlling and exploiting them and all unsuspecting people?

Righteousness is the key to unlocking the mysteries of life and it is also the key to turning your life around, whether your on the inside or the outside. You may now ask "Isn't that righteousness stuff what Jesus or Buddha or Muhammad talked about, what use is it in a messed up world like this anyway?"

The answer is that society has had a major problem in the last 2,500 years. When the Roman Catholic Church came to power and directed the Roman armies to stamp out all of the Ancient Mystical Schools they were closing the door on the higher wisdom of righteousness. They lost the keys which had been passed down to them because they were in a zealous quest to get rid of all religions except the Roman Catholic Church. We

Healing the Criminal Heart

should not put down the church itself but the leaders who, in their blindness, sentenced the world to the loss of the wonderful heritage which Jesus was trying to pass on. But where did he get his legacy of love and peace and righteousness? The answer lies in determining the origins of Christianity and then to discovering the higher sublime goals of spirituality and the means for attaining them.

All religions have a major problem. When their founder dies the people rely on scriptures and do not realize that scriptures are not alive. They must be interpreted by authentic spiritual masters. Not just by weekend preachers or intellectuals who have memorized every line of text. An authentic teaching allows you to reach the highest spiritual goals possible and an authentic Spiritual Preceptor is a person who has received the higher knowledge directly from the founder of the religion, handed down, in a succession of teacher to disciple studies. This is called the initiatic tradition and it has existed since the beginning of religion. But what is religion and what is its deeper goal and the means to attaining that goal. That is the subject of this booklet.

We will explore a six point program for turning your life around and moving in the direction of truth and prosperity. The wisdom contained here will guide you in overcoming the negativity in the world by overcoming the negativity within yourself. For who creates the world of human beings? Is it not human beings themselves? People have fashioned society and they have gotten what they have created, a world where a minority controls the wealth at the expense of the masses and where people are exploited and enslaved economically, sexually and morally.

So if there is a change to be made, if you want to make the world a better place, you must begin by turning your life around and taking the steps which will lead you to peace and inner strength. For no real change in the world is possible for the weak and weakness comes from acting, thinking and feeling in unrighteous ways.

****IMPORTANT: WHAT NEEDS TO BE DONE NEXT?

1- Begin the journey this very day. *Your first step is to purify yourself and this is done by adopting the practice of Maat Philosophy and disciplines.*
2- Practice the rituals of Neterian

When you adopt the Neterian religion you are referred to as *Shemsu Neter (Follower of God or "the Divine)*. Discover the glory of Maat and move towards the truth which is your true birthright. Leave behind the lies of the past and the negativity around you for you have all that you need right there where you are. God is waiting to touch you with the light of reason, the strength of endurance and the wisdom for success. You must turn the key by becoming a righteous instrument in the hands of God.

The Follower of Neterianism

"Shemsu Neter"

"Follower (of) Neter"

The term "Neterianism" is derived from the name "Shetaut Neter." Those who follow the spiritual path of Shetaut Neter are therefore referred to as "Neterians."

Neterianism is the science of Neter, that is, the study of the secret or mystery of Neter, the enigma of that which transcends ordinary consciousness but from which all creation arises. The world did not come from nothing, nor is it sustained by nothing. Rather it is a manifestation of that which is beyond time and space but which at the same time permeates and maintains the fundamental elements. In other words, it is the substratum of Creation and the essential nature of all that exists. So those who follow the Neter may be referred to as Neterians.

INTRODUCTION TO PART 2

THE GOAL OF THIS SECTION

In Healing The Criminal Heart Book I (Part 1 of this book) we introduced the idea that there have been many criminals in history who have become saints. We showed how they believed is a philosophy of life which brought redemption and glory to their lives and to humanity. You too can aspire to such sublime heights just as they did. The overwhelming response to book 1 has inspired the creation of this new volume for all those who would like to begin their journey from criminal to Sagehood.

The goal of this booklet is not to teach you religion or yoga philosophy although you will learn some important religious and yogic principles here. True religion and yoga cannot be learned by those who are impure. That is to say, those who have not learned how to control their lower nature. Before a person embarks of the wonderful quest of spirituality they must purify themselves. Going to a church once a week or praying before bed time is not enough. First you must understand where you are in life and how you have gotten yourself there and then a deep rooted understanding about the goal of life and the means to attaining that goal are the next tasks on the spiritual path. In fact, people who practice religion without purifying themselves are not really practicing religion in an effective way. This is why supposedly religious people fail to resist temptations and fall prey to the desires of the lower self as it is also why people who are supposedly religious do un-religious things like hurting others. Once you have incorporated the principles, presented here, into your life you can then begin to study the deeper aspects of religion and mystical philosophy. For the purpose of advanced study in this area we have prepared the books *The Wisdom of Maati, Resurrecting Osiris* and *Initiation Into Egyptian Yoga: The Secrets of Shedi.* These should all be studied at the same time.

This section will take up where *Part 1* left off. It will help you to begin the journey of spiritual enlightenment. Maat is the first and most important step because the spirit cannot manifest where there is confusion, ignorance, deceit, egoism, hatred, fear, etc. It will be your first step in the practice of Shedi.

⟶ ⌐ ⌐ , *Shedi* **(Sheti)**
"Studies into the mysteries of life"

Shedi is the Ancient Egyptian word which means to go deeply into the mysteries, to study the mystery teachings and literature profoundly, to penetrate the mysteries (spiritual discipline). It is the process of disseminating spiritual knowledge along with its correct understanding and practice to promote spiritual evolution in the individual human being as well as humanity as a whole. Shedi is not only the study of Ancient Egyptian Wisdom but also the study of world history, mythology, philosophy and religion.

WHO IS A CRIMINAL?

In Book 1 we asked this question and d the answer is that nobody is a criminal. So why are so many people in jail? Haven' crimes been committed? Aren't people being punished? What does it all mean?

There is criminal behavior but there are no criminals. Every human being is like a seed and if the seed is placed where it can get plenty of water, nutrient soil and sunlight it will grow strong and bear good fruit. If the seed is placed in a dark place where it is overshadowed by other larger trees and the soil id depleted and it needs to struggle for water and sunlight, then it will have a tough time growing and this struggle will be all that it will ever know. The seedling will grow thinking that it must do whatever it has to do to survive because nobody has shown it caring and the path to live and succeed and find the happiness of light and the prosperity of water. It will bear weak fruit and it may even bear destructive fruit in the form of hatred and anger and violence.

But is there anything wrong with the seed itself or is there something wrong with the place where it grew up and the things it learned and the painful struggle it had to go through?

There is nothing wrong with the seed and everyone is like that seed. The soul of every human being is the seed which sprouts as the human personality. If they have sprouted in a good family and learned positive attitudes and the higher goals of life they will bear wonderful fruit. If they learned to hate and to be greedy at the expense of others then they will behave as criminals.

Therefore, the soul has no stain in it because the soul is eternal but the personality is not. However, the soul suffers because it holds on to the egoism of the personality and the ego is what makes a person do evil or do good according to its level of understanding about life. If you understand life as a battle ground, a place of struggle, the dog eat dog world, etc. then you are in a very degraded state. Your actions will be selfish and if you have not found out by now, they can never lead you to true happiness, no matter how much satisfaction they may seem to bring. How better off are you for all you have stolen or for all the people you have hurt so far?

"When opulence and extravagance are a necessity instead of righteousness and truth, society will be governed by greed and injustice."

Ancient Egyptian Proverb

Everyone acts in criminal ways at some point in their life. Who has not deceived another to get something without paying? Who has not lied at some time or another? Who has not cursed another with the intent of hurting another? The difference between a criminal and a Sage is that the Sage has discovered the futility of crime and the Sage has also discovered the true purpose of life and how to discover true peace, abiding happiness and fulfillment in life. These cannot come from criminal behavior, that only leads to death and destruction, pain and sorrow. The way to truth, understanding, happiness and immortality is by the practice of virtue. Jesus said it, Muhammad said it, Lord Krishna in India said it, Buddha said it, Lao Tu said it, but it was stated with greatest emphasis and for the first time in history by Asar, the Sage or Sages in Ancient Egypt and an entire culture was based on this teaching.

> "Salvation is the freeing of the soul from its bodily fetters; becoming a God through knowledge and wisdom; controlling the forces of the cosmos instead of being a slave to them; subduing the lower nature and through awakening the higher self, ending the cycle of rebirth and dwelling with the Neters who direct and control the Great Plan."
>
> —Ancient Egyptian Proverb

In all times through history there are those who keep the light of wisdom shining for all those who are ready to embark on the journey of redemption for redemption occurs when your personality is cleansed of its ignorance and the dawn of understanding transforms you totally from an ignorant seedling who has been lost in the wilderness of life to a mighty tree of life and peace and love for all humanity.

WHAT IS RELIGION?

The term religion comes from the Latin *"Relegare"* which uses the word roots *"RE"*, which means *"BACK"*, and *"LIGON"*, which means *"to hold, to link, to bind."* Therefore, the essence of true religion is that of linking back, specifically, linking its followers back to their original source and innermost essence. In this sense the terms "religion" and "yoga" are synonymous. This source which is the underlying reality behind every object in Creation is described as unborn, undying, eternal and immortal, and is known by an endless number of names, some of which are: Consciousness, Self, Higher Self, God, Goddess, Supreme Being, Divine Self, Eternal Self, Soul, Pure Consciousness, Brahman, All, Allah, Jehovah, Neter Neteru, Creator, Absolute, Heavenly Father, Divine Mother, Great Spirit. These various names, while arising from various traditions and separate cultures, in reality represent the same divine and transcendental principle.

Although religion in its purest form is a Yoga system, the original intent and meaning of the scriptures are often misunderstood, if not distorted. This occurs because the various religions have developed in different geographic areas, and therefore, the lower levels (historical accounts, stories and traditions) have developed independently, and sometimes without proper guidance. Under these conditions, the inner meanings of the myths and symbols become lost and the exoteric meanings are emphasized. This leads to deism and a phenomenal (an occurrence or fact which is perceptible by the senses) approach to religion rather than a mystical, symbolic and transcendental understanding.

Most religions tend to be *deistic* at the elementary levels. Deism, as a religious belief or form of theism (belief in the existence of a God or gods), holds that God's action was restricted to an initial act of creation, after which He retired (separated) to contemplate the majesty of His work. Deists hold that the natural creation is regulated by laws put in place by God at the time of creation which are inscribed with perfect moral principles. Therefore, deism is closely related to the exoteric or personal understanding of the Divinity.

Myth ➔ Ritual ➔ Mysticism

Healing the Criminal Heart

In its complete form, religion is composed of three aspects, *mythology, ritual* and *metaphysical* or the *mystical experience* (mysticism - mystical philosophy). While many religions contain rituals, traditions, metaphors and myths, there are few professionals trained in understanding their deeper aspects and psychological implications (metaphysics and mystical). Thus, there is disappointment, frustration and disillusionment among many followers as well as leaders within many religions, particularly in the Western Hemisphere, because it is difficult to evolve spiritually without the proper spiritual guidance. Through introspection and spiritual research, it is possible to discover mythological vistas within religion which can rekindle the light of spirituality and at the same time increase the possibility of gaining a fuller experience of life. The exoteric (outer, ritualistic) forms of religion with which most people are familiar is only the tip of an iceberg so to speak; it is only a beginning, an invitation or prompting to seek a deeper (esoteric) discovery of the transcendental truths of existence.

> "Purification of the Heart (consciousness) leads to the Highest Good:
> Eternal Life and Supreme Peace."
> —Ancient Egyptian Proverb

All forms of spiritual practice are directed toward the goal of assisting every individual to discover the true essence of the universe both externally, in physical creation, and internally, within the human heart, as the very root of human consciousness. Thus, many terms are used to describe the attainment of the goal of spiritual knowledge and the eradication of spiritual ignorance. Some of these terms are: *Enlightenment, Resurrection, Salvation, The Kingdom of Heaven, Moksha or Liberation, Buddha Consciousness, One With The Tao, Self-realization, to Know Thyself,* etc.

Religion and Yoga

Yoga is the practice of mental, physical and spiritual disciplines which lead to self-control and self-discovery by purifying the mind, body and spirit, so as to discover the deeper spiritual essence which lies within every human being and object in the universe. In essence, the goal of yoga practice is to unite or *yoke* one's individual consciousness with universal or cosmic consciousness. Therefore, Ancient Egyptian religious practice, especially in terms of the rituals and other practices of the Ancient Egyptian temple system known as *Shetaut Neter* (the way of the hidden Supreme Being), may be termed as a yoga system: *Egyptian Yoga.* In this sense, religion, in its purest form, is a yoga system, as it seeks to reunite people with their true and original source.

The disciplines of Yoga fall under five major categories. These are: *Yoga of Wisdom, Yoga of Devotional Love, Yoga of Meditation, Tantric Yoga* and *Yoga of Selfless Action.* Within these categories there are subsidiary forms which are part of the main disciplines. The emphasis in the Osirian Myth is on the Yoga of Wisdom, Yoga of Devotional Love and Yoga of Selfless Action. The important point to remember is that all aspects of yoga can and should be used in an integral fashion to effect an efficient and harmonized spiritual movement in the practitioner. While a yogin may place emphasis on the Yoga of Wisdom, they may also practice Devotional Yoga and Meditation Yoga along with the wisdom studies.

So the practice of any discipline that leads to oneness with Supreme Consciousness can be called yoga. If you study, rationalize and reflect upon the teachings, you are practicing *Yoga of Wisdom*. If you meditate upon the teachings and your Higher Self, you are practicing *Yoga of Meditation*. If you practice rituals which identify you with your spiritual nature, you are practicing *Yoga of Ritual Identification* (which is part of the Yoga of Wisdom and the Yoga of Devotional Love of the Divine). If you develop your physical nature and psychic energy centers, you are practicing *Serpent Power* (*Kundalini or Uraeus*) *Yoga* (which is part of Tantric Yoga). If you practice living according to the teachings of ethical behavior and selflessness, you are practicing *Yoga of Action* (Maat) in daily life. If you practice turning your attention towards the Divine by developing love for the Divine, then it is called *Devotional Yoga* or *Yoga of Divine Love*. The practitioner of yoga is called a yogin (male practitioner) or yogini (female practitioner), and one who has attained the culmination of yoga (union with the Divine) is called a yogi. In this manner, yoga has been developed into many disciplines which may be used in an integral fashion to achieve the same goal: Enlightenment. Therefore, the aspirant should learn about all of the paths of yoga and choose those elements which best suit his/her personality or practice them all in an integral, balanced way.

Enlightenment is the term used to describe the highest level of spiritual awakening. It means attaining such a level of spiritual awareness that one discovers the underlying unity of the entire universe as well as the fact that the source of all creation is the same source from which the innermost Self within every human heart arises.

The scriptures and teachings serve the purpose of enlightening those who have discovered that there is a deeper basis to life other than what is promoted by the general society. The Sages of ancient times created the scriptures to assist those who would like to discover this inner reality and would be otherwise lost in the wilderness of ignorance and suffering which constitutes ordinary human life.

DEFINITIONS

SHETAUT NETER: THE NAME OF **OUR RELIGION**

The Sema Institute of Yoga teaches the Shetaut Neter Religion. *Shetaut Neter* meaning: "The Way of the Hidden Supreme Being." This is the oldest known religion in human history and it originated in Ancient Egypt prior to 5,000 B.C.E. The practice of Shetaut Neter is given in the teachings of Smai Taui and Maat Philosophy which was authored by African peoples in 5,000 B.C.E. or earlier.

SMAI-TAUI, "EGYPTIAN YOGA" AND MAAT PHILOSOPHY

SMAI-TAUI is the Ancient Egyptian word and symbol meaning *spiritual union*, which is known in modern times as the discipline of YOGA. What is Yoga? The literal meaning of the word YOGA is to *"YOKE"* or to *"LINK"* back. The implication is: to link back individual consciousness to its original source, the original essence: Universal

Consciousness. UAA (meditation) and MAAT (ethics and righteaous thinking, speaking and acting) are the disciplines called SHEDI which allow a person to realize the goals of Egyptian Yoga. Yoga philosophy originated at the dawn of civilization in the present era of human history beginning with the emergence of ancient Egyptian civilization. The Ancient Egyptians influenced European, Indian and other African Religions and is therefore, relevant to every human being. The main purposed for the existence of the Sema Institute is to bring forth the useful principles of Ancient Egyptian Maat philosophy which is the main form in which Egyptian Yoga is practiced.

〰️〰️〰️, **Maat,** "Truth, Righteousness, Order, Harmony"

MAAT is the Ancient Egyptian philosophy of righteous living based on the most ancient wisdom teachings created by the Sages of Kamit (Ancient Egypt) over 5,000 years ago who wrote the oldest books in our history that contain the wisdom of the art of righteous living. It refers to a deep understanding of the manner in which virtuous qualities can be developed in the human heart so as to come closer to oneness with family, community, society, humanity and the universe. Maat philosophy is a spiritual philosophy similar to the philosophy of Dharma in Indian Buddhism or the Tao of Chinese Taoism but it predates these by several thousands of years. Maat is a philosophy, a spiritual symbol as well as a cosmic energy or force which pervades the entire universe. Maat is the embodiment of world order, justice, righteousness, correctness, harmony and peace. Maat represents wisdom and spiritual awakening through balance, equanimity, meditation and ethical living and the promotion of justice, harmony and ethics in society.

What are Yoga Philosophy and Ancient Egyptian Mystical Spirituality?

Yoga is an ancient art of spiritual living that began in Ancient Egypt. Technically, Yoga is not a religion but religions do use yoga disciplines such as chanting, meditation, etc. Yoga Philosophy is the essence of all religions. Therefore, no matter what religion you were brought up with, Christianity, Islam, Hinduism, Judaism, Shetaut Neter, etc., if you practice the principles of Yoga you will gain greater insight into your religion. Therefore, Yoga does not conflict with any religion but it enhances it. Most people think of spirituality and of God in terms of sectarian forms traditionally passed on by religious organizations. The Supreme Divinity is often seen as a powerful yet fearsome being who sends people to eternal damnation. However, in the light of Yoga philosophy and through the various disciplines developed by the yogic masters over the last 7,000 years, the Supreme Divinity is to be understood in a much more universal way. We not only discover the infinite compassion and love of the Self (Supreme Divinity) but through the various practices of Yoga, which have been tailored for the various levels of human spiritual development and different personalities, it is also possible to partake in the glory of Divinity. This is the goal of Yoga.

Healing the Criminal Heart

No matter how low a human being goes in his/her existence, the practice of Yoga with the correct understanding supplies a sure way to overcome any and all human ills, frailties and failings. This is true because all individuals are essentially one with the Divine Self. Through a process of ignorance they have forgotten their true identity. Through the process of Yoga, you may discover your true essence, thereby unleashing the gifts and infinite power of the soul.

With this inner power which comes from wisdom and self effort toward cleansing the heart from its negative emotions, feelings and thoughts, anyone can overcome incredible obstacles. This is the power that made it possible for the Ancient Egyptians to create the massive pyramids and temples out of stone without machinery. They were able to accomplish feats of engineering which modern society cannot duplicate. Even more importantly, they developed a science of spiritual development which has influenced all world religions and in the Egyptian Yoga Book Series, we show how the Ancient Egyptian elements are still present in Christianity, Islam, Hinduism, Buddhism and Taoism.

The heart of this science of self improvement is known to the world as *Yoga*. In recent times Yoga has been made popular by the Indian practitioners. In our book series we have shown that Indian Yoga is a continuation of the same teaching which was given in Ancient Egypt and that in ancient times Africa (where Egypt is located) was culturally connected to India. Many people have been introduced to yoga as a practice of physical exercise for health and relaxation, but in reality, Yoga is much more than that. Physical health and relaxation are only the beginning stage of yoga which is necessary in order to make it possible for a practitioner to understand and practice the higher teachings of self-development. Yoga is a vast science of self development which has proven its effectiveness over the last 7,000 years.

The Pursuit of Happiness

General society believes that actions are to be performed for the goal of attaining some objective which will yield a reward. The socialization process teaches the individual to seek to perform actions because this is the way to attain something which will cause happiness. This is the predicament of the masses of people who have not studied Yoga or Mystical Philosophies such as Buddhism, Shetaut Neter or Vedanta. The following line from the Declaration of Independence illustrates this point succinctly.

> We hold these truths to be self-evident, that all men are created equal,
> that they are endowed by their Creator with certain unalienable Rights,
> that among these are Life, Liberty and the **pursuit of Happiness**.

Yoga philosophy is not against the pursuit of happiness in the world of time and space, however, it does teach that the pursuit of happiness with a sense of attachment and dependence on objects and situations in the world of human experience will inevitably lead to disappointment and frustration and will not fulfill the deeper need of the soul. If at all they should be pursued with an attitude of detachment and dispassion. In reality, happiness does not and cannot come from objects that can be acquired or from activities that are performed. It can only come from within. Even actions that seem to be pleasurable in life cannot be considered as a source of happiness from a philosophical point of view because all activities are relative. This means that one activity is pleasurable for one person and painful for another. This leads to the realization that it is not the activity itself that holds the happiness but the individual doer who is performing the action and assigning a value to it which she or he has learned from society to assign. Therefore, if it was learned that going out to a party is supposed to be fun then that activity will be pursued as a source of happiness. Here action is performed in pursuit of the fruit of the action in the form happiness; a result is desired from the action. However, there are several negative psychological factors which arise that will not allow true happiness to manifest. The first is that the relentless pursuit of the action renders the mind restless and agitated. The second is that if the activity is not possible there will be depression in the mind. If the activity is thwarted by some outside force, meaning that something or someone prevented you from achieving the object or activity you saw as the "source of happiness" you develop anger toward it. If by chance you succeed in achieving the object or activity you become elated and this will cause greed in the mind, you will want more and more of it. When you are not able to get more at any particular time you will become depressed and disappointed. Therefore, under these conditions a constant dependence on outside activities and worldly objects develops in the mind which will not allow for peace and contentment. Even though it is illogical to pursue activities which cause pain in life people are constantly acting against their own interests as they engage in actions in an effort to gain happiness while in reality they are enhancing the probability of encountering pain later on. People often act and shortly regret what they have done. Sometimes people know even at the time of their actions that they are wrong and yet they are unable to stop themselves. This is because when the mind is controlled by desires and expectations the intellect, the light of reason, is *clouded* and *dull*. However, when the mind is controlled by the intellect, then it is not possible to be led astray due to the *fantasies* and *illusions* of the mind. When the individual is guided by their intellect, then only right actions can be performed no matter what negative ideas arise in the mind. Such a person can not be deluded into negative actions and when negative actions (actions which lead to future pain and disappointments) are not performed then unhappiness cannot exist. Thus, a person who lives according to the teachings of non-doership (without desire or expectations for the future results of their actions) lives a life of perpetual peace and happiness in the present.

Thus, true peace and inner fulfillment will never come through pursuit of actions when there is an expectation or desire for the fruits of those actions. The belief in objects or worldly activities as a source of happiness if therefore seen as a state known as *ignorance* wherein the individual is caught up in the *illusions*, *fantasies* and *fanciful notions* of the mind. However, happiness and peace can arise spontaneously when there is an attitude of detachment and dispassion toward objects and situations in life. If actions are performed with the idea of discovering peace within, based on the understanding of the philosophy outlined above, and for the sake of the betterment of society, then these actions will have the effect of purifying the heart of the individual. The desires and expectations will dwindle while the inner fulfillment and awareness of the present moment will increase. There will be greater and greater discovery of peace within; a discovery of what is truly stable and changeless within as opposed to the mind and outer world which are constantly changing and unpredictable. Along with this there is greater effectiveness and perfection in one's actions.

The Source of Pain In Life

Misery in life stems from the ignorance of one's true nature. Human beings are like kings or queens who wander around the countryside as beggars, not knowing their true identity. They act as beggars, treat others unkindly, indulge in hatred and anger of others, and they are internally frustrated due to their condition but don't know what to do about it so they go on from day to day wasting their lives thinking that there is no hope. You are unaware of your talents and of your capacity to love yourself and others. You have come to a state which has led you to experience the degradation and loss of spiritual and physical freedom. You search for excitement and fulfillment of your desires through your worldly relationships, by entertaining yourself with the media, drugs or alcohol, or by acquiring objects (cars, clothes, etc.) that you think will make you happy. You do these things because you have been taught that this is the way to pursue happiness. But have any of these things brought you true and lasting happiness and peace? Do you know anyone who has found abiding happiness in this way? Why is it that once you get something you wanted it only satisfies you for a short while? Why is it that physical pleasure and comfort also only satisfy you for a short while? And before you know it you are again searching for something else. Its like a drug and society is hooked on it and society is out of control. Why are there commercials constantly telling you to buy some car, drink, food, etc. to make yourself happy? Why is there constant pressure to use some shampoo or lotion or style to look good or cool or hip or in style, etc.? If this was the answer surely somebody should have discovered whatever there is to buy in order to be happy should they not? Those who suffer most are the people who can least control themselves. There is no object to buy and no person who can give you all you need to become truly happy. Only you can discover that for yourself if you understand the secret of life. Otherwise you are doomed to continue in the cycle of crime and punishment not just in this lifetime but in future lifetimes as well. This means that if you do not correct the spiritual ignorance in your personality and move on the path of purifying your heart, you will end up in the same place again and again.

In order to be truly happy you must unleash your spirit. You must rediscover the seed state in your being, that innocence which is the true essence of every human being. Yoga can help you to discover this essence of beauty and glory within. You are the one responsible for your condition because of your past actions based on ignorance. Therefore, do not waste any more time by blaming others or by seeking to find explanations in society or other external causes. The wonderful thing is that you are also the one who, by your actions illumined by the light of wisdom in action (Maat), can change your life.

THE SOLUTION TO THE PROBLEM

The Ancient Egyptians prescribed one solution to all of the problems of life and they built an entire country based on this concept. Its legacy lives on up to this day. The solution is to *Know Thyself*. Through self knowledge, all of the misconceptions of the mind which have led to degraded states, erroneous thoughts, conflict and misunderstanding, violence, hatred, greed, etc. are washed away. Through self knowledge one discovers the supreme happiness which comes from inner contentment and peace that cannot come from external objects or relationships in the world. When you know your true self you will be a new personality and completely redeemed from your past.

Your interest (reading this volume) indicates that you have begun to recognize that there is a higher goal in life for you other than your current experience. This is a blessing because most people are not able to see the misery of their own condition and then to do something about it. Most people are caught in the web of negativity they have woven in their minds and go on like robots from one miserable situation to another. Your task is to follow up on this interest, study the teachings and begin practicing them in your life right now. Develop a relationship with your inner Higher Self and discover the strength to overcome your failings and thereby lead yourself to a better life, prosperity, peace and enlightenment. Everyone is a child of the Divine, as such everyone is capable of supreme good according to their level of awareness of their true self. Those who are most degraded, demoralized, humiliated and abused as well as those who are most egocentric, arrogant, who like to cause terror and violence are the ones who are farthest away from the truth even though they may be appearing to enjoy causing hurt and fear in reality they are hurting inside and running away from the truth in fear.

Many people do not understand God and so they have come to believe that they are dammed and that they are going to hell for what they have done. This is a lie handed out by a society which does not want to face its sickness of greed and sexuality. Our society is convinced that promoting the lower self in everyone is the best way to have prosperity. This is why there is constant advertising with sex and celebrities. But how many people can have plastic surgery to look like the TV models or movie superstars? Why is it that everyday you can pick up a paper and see some rich Hollywood Star going into rehab doe to a drug problem or being arrested for violence (domestic or otherwise). How much more will you need to see before you realize that the ordinary values of society are not only against spirituality but also against human life itself? They are destructive to people, animals and the environment and the shocking rise in the amounts of people who are incarcerated should tell someone that there is a serious problem and yet their answer is to build more jails.

However, just as a plant must receive the proper nutrients (soil, water, sunlight, etc.) so too the human heart must receive the proper caring and nurturing in the form of love, wisdom, proper diet, meditation and good will.

THE ROAD OF MAAT

In Ancient Egypt there was a keen understanding of life's struggle. It is a struggle about righteousness and unrighteousness. Righteousness was called Maat and unrighteousness was called N-Maat. The Ancient Egyptian Sages notices over many years that when a person performs certain actions they set other events in motion and ultimately those events have an effect on the world which ultimately comes back to the person who performed the original action. This came to be known as the law of cause and effect. The Sages also noticed that most people do not realize that this law exists. It is everywhere in nature and yet people go on blindly acting and receiving the fruits of their actions, some good and some bad. They also discovered that positive and negative circumstances follow a person even after death. A person could go to discover God after death if they performed certain actions while alive. This came to be known as heaven, the supreme good, *Nefer*. But a person could also experience fear frustration, anguish, pain and sorrow after death as well if they have performed negative actions. This came to be known as hell. But it does not end there. After experiencing hellish conditions after death the soul comes back to the earth to life again in another body. This is called reincarnation and it is all based on a person's actions.

From their standpoint, as Sages, they realized that realizing the existence of this universal law they could act in certain ways that would allow them to avoid the negative consequences and to promote the positive consequences. They learned how to promote prosperity and to avoid adversity in life, as well as after death. They recorded their knowledge and called it Maat ⟿ ⟀ ◯ ⸮ . Maat is that straightness and rectitude in life which leads to the highest blessedness. Maat is the reason why Ancient Egyptian Society survived for thousands of years and did not suffer the fate of decadent societies such as Rome, Babylon, etc. In Ancient Egypt the judges, lawyers and police were all initiated into the teachings of Maat. Consequently, any judge taking bribes, any lawyer attempting to deceive the court, any government official attempting to make laws to favor some people and not others and any police person who violated the rights of the citizens would be severely punished and stripped of their job. This was the seriousness with which the discipline of law was taken. Why? Because human beings are God's children, all of them, no matter where they come from, no matter if they are male or female, young or old. This means that they are all Divine essentially and should be treated with the respect accorded to royalty.

The Status of Women in Ancient Egypt

This is why in Ancient Egypt women had equal rights under the law. Women enjoyed such equal status that they were respected in and out of their family. This respect allowed the ancient Egyptian family to be strong. Men who did not remain true to their wives were dealt with not only by consequences from the law but they would lose the respect of society. In modern times adultery and promiscuity are promoted as a great lifestyle but has nobody noticed the degraded society it has led to? In Ancient Egypt women could walk around bare breasted like the men and not have any fear of rape or lustful looks. Rape would have been considered a great crime and lewd and lascivious behavior would have been considered disrespectful and a sign of mental illness.

The highest law of the land was the Pharaoh. The Pharaoh had the responsibility to keep Maat on earth as God kept it in heave and by doing this peace and prosperity could be maintained indefinitely. Therefore, the Pharaoh was respected and assisted in the task of upholding order in society and order cannot exist without justice. If the Pharaoh did not exemplify the best in spiritual principles and justice he or she would not be able to rule. In modern times lewd and lascivious behavior in public figures, even in leaders, is accepted and promoted so is there any wonder why there is no respect for women and the family units are breaking down? Is there any wonder why in 1998 the divorce rate for first marriages is 65% and second marriages is 80% and worst for third time marriages?

For these reasons and many more Ancient Egyptian civilization lasted so very long. If you want to rise above the injustice of the world you must eradicate any injustice in your own mind, your own dealings and actions. If you want top promote peace in your environment and in the world you must eradicate all traces of violence, hatred and greed from yourself. In order to rise above the injustice of the world you must become justice and truth and peace. Otherwise you will be swept up in the madness of the world and you will never discover how to achieve real happiness.

THE IMPORTANCE OF MAAT IN SOCIETY

The Ancient Egyptian teachings of Maat talk about the *Fetters of the soul*. This teaching holds that ordinary human consciousness, the soul, is beset with gross impurities which must be overcome before advanced spiritual disciplines can be practiced successfully. These impurities are known as: ignorance, anger, hate, greed, jealousy, passion, etc. Until the gross impurities are controlled, it will not be possible to progress on the path of advanced yoga instruction. Control of the gross impurities is accomplished through the practice of righteous living, what Indian Yoga calls *Dharma* or what Ancient Egyptian Yoga calls *Maat*. Both of these terms signify the practice of righteous living and of course this is the same goal of the Christian *Beatitudes*, the teachings that Jesus gave in the Sermon on the Mount. Righteousness acts to purify a person because when a person practices living in accordance with truth they cannot also act in egoistic ways. Self knowledge is the highest goal of righteousness. Righteousness is therefore everything done for the sake of moving towards self-knowledge. Unrighteousness is any movement that takes a person away from self-knowledge. When you study the teachings, practice meditation, help another, your heart expands and you feel your connectedness with others and with the universe. When you hurt others you are acting egoistically and you are pulling away from the universe and into your little ego self. This is why selfishness and revenge seem to bring pleasure in the short run but in the long term they are painful. When you act hatefully and vengefully you are actually hurting yourself by hurting that other person because deep down all souls are united in God, not the personality with its egoism and ignorance, but the soul deep down. This is the great secret that the Sages have discovered and this is why they tell people not to be greedy and that they should share. When you do not share you are closing off your own heart and unconsciously you begin to turn against yourself and lead yourself to negative situations and this your own punishment for yourself.

When you practice righteousness you are actually putting down the ego, with its ignorance and wrong ways, and allowing yourself to discover your soul and its gifts. Therefore, the ego becomes less and less important and the mind, unburdened by the desires of the ego, becomes clearer and sensitive to the spiritual wisdom. This is when a person begins to display the latent artistic gifts, creativity and great works. As long as a person is caught up in their ego they will never do truly great things in life. The best they will do is to get by and they will suffer in the process. Another important aspect of spiritual practice is *Shedi* (keeping company of sages-good association). Shedi helps a person to overcome obstacles in the practice of the teachings and to understand the deeper meaning of the teachings. Shedi is an advanced spiritual studies group. Working in a group with others who are interested, as you are, will facilitate your understanding and give you enthusiasm in your practice. Therefore, wherever you go meet with others, who are interested, and set up Shedi study groups.

The practice of Maat is the discovery of the virtuous qualities within you and the shedding of the ignorance and error which you have learned in this and previous lifetimes. In reality you have a virtuous soul and it is yearning to be discovered and this is why you are reading this book this very moment. Therefore, do not be discouraged because of your crimes or your negative thoughts or feelings. Your higher Self is ready and willing to forgive these and to welcome you with open arms to the ranks of those who want to discover true peace, contentment and happiness.

THE FORMS OF RA

In order for this process of purification and self-discovery to begin you must place yourself in the hands of the goddess (Maat). Allow her to receive you and to comfort you and guide you. We will concentrate our beginning studies on the six main principles of the 42 Precepts of Maat. The six principles should be studied in an in depth group setting. They 42 precepts should be read daily, at dawn, noon time and at dusk. This three-fold spiritual practice brings order to your day by harmonizing you with the three phases of Ra, who manifests as the sun. Ra is the Supreme Being in Ancient Egyptian Mythology. He has three aspects or forms and each serves to sustain life but they also relate to important mystical teachings. Here we will only explore some of these.   Ra's first form, the morning sun is called Khepra. This is the dawning of a new life. So every morning you must begin your spiritual practices with the ideal of creating a new life as you create each new day. Activity: Morning prayers and meditations.

Ra's second manifestation, the noon time sun, is called Ra (or Ra-heru, Atum-Ra, Amun-Ra). This is the sustaining of a new life. So every midday you must renew your vows and seek the light within you in silent meditation on the higher self which is sustaining you at every moment. Life is not sustained by food but by the life force energy of the sun. If the sun were to stop shining there would be a cessation of all life no matter how much food you have or how much electricity you have. Activity: Noon prayers and meditations.

Ra's third manifestation, the setting sun, is called Tem. This is the culmination of life, the reaching of your goals, the accomplishment of what you have set out to do in that day. A job well done allows you to sleep well. Do something constructive, gain a skill that you can use to support yourself righteously, get your high school diploma, teach others, help others with the spirit of allowing the goddess, Maat, to work through your. So every evening reassess your goals and your accomplishments and give thanks for the opportunity to serve. For in serving others you are really serving yourself because the service itself requires you to sublimate what is negative into what is good and the more good feeling you have the more the goddess is drawn to you in the form of prosperity and peace.

MAAT AND RA

In a grander sense the three forms of Ra represent the three stages of life, Birth, Adulthood, Old age-death. The key to understanding this cycle is in the mythology of goddess Maat.

MAAT is the daughter of Ra, the high God, thus in a hymn to Ra we find:

> *The land of Manu* (the West) *receives thee with satisfaction, and the goddess MAAT embraces thee both at morn and at eve... the god*

Tehuti and the goddess MAAT have written down thy daily course for thee every day...

Another Hymn in the Papyrus of Qenna provides deeper insight into MAAT. Qenna says:

I have come to thee, O Lord of the Gods, Temu-Heru-khuti, whom MAAT directeth... Amun-Ra rests upon MAAT... Ra lives by MAAT... Osiris carries along the earth in His train by MAAT...

MAAT is the *daughter of Ra,* and she was with him on His celestial barque when he first emerged from the primeval waters along with His company of gods and goddesses. She is also known as the *eye of Ra, lady of heaven, queen of the earth, mistress of the Underworld and the lady of the gods and goddesses.* MAAT also has a dual form or *MAATI.* In her *capacity* of God, MAAT is *Shes MAAT* which means *ceaseless-ness and regularity* of the course of the sun (i.e. the universe). In the form of MAATI, she represents the South and the North which symbolize Upper and Lower Egypt as well as the Higher and Lower Self. MAAT is the personification of justice and righteousness upon which God has created the universe and MAAT is also the essence of God and creation. Therefore, it is MAAT who judges the soul when it arrives in the judgment hall of MAAT. Sometimes MAAT herself becomes the scales upon which the heart of the initiate is judged. MAAT judges the heart (unconscious mind) of the initiate in an attempt to determine to what extent the heart has lived in accordance with MAAT or truth, correctness, reality, genuineness, uprightness, righteousness, justice, steadfastness and the unalterable nature of creation.

Chapter 125 of The Book of Coming Forth By Day and the 42 Precepts of Maat

Though the Ancient Egyptian Book of Coming Forth By Day is the most popular text of Ancient Egypt it must be understood that the Wisdom Texts are the source of the teachings presented in the Book of Coming Forth By Day. The teachings expressed in the Book of Coming Forth By Day known as the 42 precepts of Maat are in reality a culmination or an affirmation of a life lived according to righteous conduct and spiritual wisdom. The Wisdom Texts date back to the period of 5,000 B.C.E. known as the "Old Kingdom" period of Dynastic Egypt and represent the earliest known examples of instructions in the art of living for harmony in society and for spiritual evolution. They were copied upon temple walls and papyruses and were designed for the general instruction of the Ancient Egyptian population.

In Chapter 125 of the Ancient Egyptian Book of Coming Forth By Day it is stated that one should be able to declare one's innocence from wrong doing in order to see the face of God and com into Gods presence. How is this possible? Can a human being aspire to perfection and divine vision? The Wisdom Texts show how this is possible in language and instructions which are relevant to modern times. The teachings are universal and therefore applicable to all human beings regardless of the country of origin, the religious affiliation, the gender, the age, etc.

Healing the Criminal Heart

Through the practice of the precepts of Maat, mental peace and subtlety of intellect (purity of heart) arise. Purity of heart, meaning the eradication of or anger, hatred, greed, jealousy, discontent, covetousness, elation, stress, agitation, etc. from the heart. The heart in spiritual literature, means the mind and personality. This is the means through which divine awareness is possible. When the mind is beset with agitation it is impossible to develop spiritual sensitivity. The mind in this state is as if caught in a web of illusion based on the thoughts, desires and ignorance which do not allow awareness of the Divine essence within the heart or in nature, but rather intensify the feelings of individualism, separation and individuality along with the negative aspects of your personality (anger, hatred, greed, jealousy, etc.). These in turn open the door for feelings egoistic or personal desires to arise. Feelings of animosity, anger, hatred, greed, jealousy, lust, elation, depression, etc. can only exist when there is individuality or egoism (ignorance).

Think about it, can you feel jealous of your arm, your head, your foot? No because these are part of you. They are an integral part of your being. In the same way, a perfected (righteous) Sage or Saint sees the entire universe as his or her body and therefore cannot feel jealous, angry, greedy, etc. towards anything or anyone. Can you be angry with your teeth for biting your tongue by mistake? Then you should not be angry with those who hurt you because they are doing it out of ignorance. You should always try to protect yourself. Non-violence does not mean allowing others to hurt you physically. This would be humiliation and it is not conducive to spiritual growth. Humility means seeing a grander vision of life, understanding that in the big picture there is a grander truth which most people are unaware of and because of this vision you stop looking at yourself with conceit and arrogance but with caring and compassion. This is possible because the feelings of ignorance, individuality and separation have been replaced with truth and universality. Now there is equal vision towards all and universal love for all that exists. This is the experience of an enlightened human being.

The Precepts of Maat are to be read, chanted or written daily. This is especially true of chapter 125 of Book of Coming Forth By Day. In this manner they are to be studied and practiced so as to engender a mind that is peaceful and harmonious. In this peace and harmony they will transform the mind and lead it to what is positive and good.

The following is a composite summary of "negative confessions" from several Ancient Egyptian *Books of Coming Forth by Day*. While all of these books include 42 precepts, some specific precepts varied according to the specific initiate for which they were prepared and the priests who compiled them. Therefore, I have included more than one precept per line where I felt it was appropriate to show that there were slight variations in the precepts and to more accurately reflect the broader view of the original texts. They should be recited daily and their meaning should be meditated upon and practiced daily.

(1) "I have not done iniquity." Variant: Acting with falsehood.
(2) "I have not robbed with violence."
(3) "I have not done violence (To anyone or anything)." Variant: Rapacious (Taking by force; plundering.)
(4) "I have not committed theft." Variant: Coveted.

(5) "I have not murdered man or woman." <u>Variant: Or ordered someone else to commit murder.</u>

(6) "I have not defrauded offerings." <u>Variant: or destroyed food supplies or increased or decreased the measures to profit.</u>

(7) "I have not acted deceitfully." <u>Variant: With crookedness.</u>

(8) "I have not robbed the things that belong to God."

(9) "I have told no lies."

(10) "I have not snatched away food."

(11) "I have not uttered evil words." <u>Variant: Or allowed myself to become sullen, to sulk or become depressed.</u>

(12) "I have attacked no one."

(13) "I have not slaughtered the cattle that are set apart for the Gods." <u>Variant: The Sacred bull – (Apis)</u>

(14) "I have not eaten my heart" (overcome with anguish and distraught). <u>Variant: Committed perjury.</u>

(15) "I have not laid waste the ploughed lands."

(16) "I have not been an eavesdropper or pried into matters to make mischief." <u>Variant: Spy.</u>

(17) "I have not spoken against anyone." <u>Variant: Babbled, gossiped.</u>

(18) "I have not allowed myself to become angry without cause."

(19) "I have not committed adultery." <u>Variant: And homosexuality.</u>

(20) "I have not committed any sin against my own purity."

(21) "I have not violated sacred times and seasons."

(22) "I have not done that which is abominable."

(23) "I have not uttered fiery words. I have not been a man or woman of anger."

(24) "I have not stopped my ears against the words of right and wrong (Maat)."

(25) "I have not stirred up strife (disturbance)." "I have not caused terror." "I have not struck fear into any man."

(26) "I have not caused any one to weep." <u>Variant: Hoodwinked.</u>

(27) "I have not lusted or committed fornication nor have I lain with others of my same sex." <u>Variant: or sex with a boy.</u>

(28) "I have not avenged myself." <u>Variant: Resentment.</u>

(29) "I have not worked grief, I have not abused anyone." <u>Variant: Quarrelsome nature.</u>

(30) "I have not acted insolently or with violence."

(31) "I have not judged hastily." <u>Variant: or been impatient.</u>

(32) "I have not transgressed or angered God."

(33) "I have not multiplied my speech overmuch (talk too much)."

(34) "I have not done harm or evil." <u>Variant: Thought evil.</u>

(35) "I have not worked treason or curses on the King."

(36) "I have never befouled the water." <u>Variant: held back the water from flowing in its season.</u>

(37) "I have not spoken scornfully." <u>Variant: Or yelled unnecessarily or raised my voice.</u>

(38) "I have not cursed The God."

(39) "I have not behaved with arrogance." <u>Variant: Boastful.</u>

(40) "I have not been overwhelmingly proud or sought for distinctions for myself (Selfishness)."

(41) "I have never magnified my condition beyond what was fitting or increased my wealth, except with such things as are (justly) mine own possessions by means of Maat." <u>Variant: I have not disputed over possessions except when they concern my own rightful possessions. Variant: I have not desired more than what is rightfully mine.</u>

(42) "I have never thought evil (blasphemed) or slighted The God in my native town."

SUMMATION OF THE 42 PRECEPTS

The 42 declarations of purity have profound implications for the spiritual development of the individual as well as for society. There are six important principles contained in the precepts of Maat from the Ancient Egyptian Book of Coning Forth By Day. They must be learned well and incorporated into each aspect of your life. They may be grouped under three basic ethical teachings, *Truth, Non-violence* and *Self Control.* Under the heading of self-control, three subheadings may be added, *Balance of Mind or Right Thinking Based on Reason, Non-stealing* and *Sex-Sublimation.* Each number to the right of the virtue corresponds to the line in the precept list.

> Truth 1, 6, 8, 15, 18, 22, 26, 27, 34
> Non-violence 2, 4, 5, 10 , 12, 14, 23, 25, 29, 33,
> Self-Control-Right Action 10, 16, 17, 22, 24, 25, 28, 31, 32, 35, 37, 39
> Balance of Mind-reason, 13, 19, 26, 30, 36, 38,
> Not-stealing 3, 6, 7, 9, 40, 41, 42
> Sex-Sublimation 11, 20, 21

There is one important factor which is inherent in the precepts of Maat that must receive special mention. Many times when people are ignorant of the greater spiritual realities and caught up in the emotionality of human life they tend to look for something to blame for their miseries. They want to find a cause for the troubles of life and the easiest way to do this is to look around into the world and point to those factors around them which seem to affect them. In Chapter 125 the use of the word *nuk* ("I") is emphasized with a special connotation. The spiritual aspirant says continually "I have not...". He or she does not say "you have allowed me" or "the devil made me do it" or "I wanted to but I couldn't", etc.

There is a process of responsibility wherein the spiritual aspirant recognizes that he or she has the obligation to act righteously and in so doing to purify their own heart. Spiritual practice can succeed only when you assume responsibility for your actions, thoughts, words and feelings. If you constantly blame your adversities on others or on situations, etc. you will be living life according to ignorance and weakness. True spiritual strength comes from leaning upon the Self within for spiritual support and well being rather than upon external situations, people or objects.

Thus within the teachings of MAAT can be found all of the important injunctions for living a life which promotes purity, harmony and sanctity. While these may be found in other spiritual traditions from around the world, seldom is the emphasis on non-violence and balance to be found. In Christianity Jesus emphasized non-violence and in Buddhism Buddha emphasized non-violence. These traditions recognized the power of non-violence to heal the anger and hatred within the aggressor as well as the victim and when this spiritual force is developed it is more formidable that any kind of physical violence. Therefore, anyone who wishes to promote peace and harmony in the world must begin by purifying every bit of negativity within themselves. This is the only way to promote harmony and peace in others. Conversely, if there is anger within you are indeed promoting anger outside of yourself and your efforts will be unsuccessful in the end.

HOW TO UNDERSTAND AND PRACTICE THE SIX PRINCIPLES OF MAAT

Remember that virtue is not something you acquire. Virtue is an expression of the level of spiritual sensitivity you have because virtue is your true nature. So the closer you get to your higher Self the more virtuousness you discover within yourself. Evil and negativity arise when there is ignorance of the Self. As you discover your true Self you will also discover the glory, power and virtue that is in you. The task is then to discover your virtue. The process of self discovery occurs through righteous action. Righteous Action is virtuous action and as you act virtuously you will become your virtuous self and be freed from the degradation, humiliation and pain of feeling like a failure or a worthless human being. You are a child of God as the Ancient Egyptian proverbs boldly proclaim. As such there is no real negativity in you if only you discover the truth of you real Self.

The following essays are provided as study group guides for discussion. They should be read and then discussed by the group. Bring up situations from the day or from past experiences and determine what was the incorrect action and what is proper action for the future. As you study each principle you should also recite the corresponding lines in the list of 42 Precepts and discuss them individually. If you do not finish one principle in the allotted time pick up where you left off at your next meeting. Do not proceed to the next principle until you review the precepts. When you finish the sixth principle begin again with the first. You will discover deeper issues as you go over them a second time around. You can also bring in pertinent points from your other readings in the book series.

PRINCIPLE ONE:
REFLECTIONS ON TRUTH
(Precepts 1, 6, 8, 15, 18, 22, 26, 27, 34)

"The fool who does not hear, can do nothing at all; looking at ignorance and seeing knowledge; looking at harmfulness and seeing usefulness; living on the things by which one dies; the food of evil speech."
—Ancient Egyptian Proverb

Healing the Criminal Heart

The root cause of vice in the human personality is ignorance of one's true identity as being one with the Self (God). Otherwise there would be no desire to acquire objects that you don't need and no need to hate what obstructs your movement to acquire what is desired or a need to love and become attached to what seems to bring pleasure because in self-knowledge there is peace, contentment and fulfillment. Without self-knowledge (the state of ignorance) there is always something missing, always a need to seek fulfillment. These needs give rise to the myriad forms of desire which arise in the human heart. The deep rotted desires of the human heart wear down a human being's ability to act with reason and righteousness. The will is weakened and negative actions become accepted and sanctioned by the weak will. This was first understood and explained in the Ancient Egyptian Wisdom Text writings known as "TEACHINGS OF PTAHOTEP":

> The fool who does not hear,
> He can do nothing at all;
> He sees knowledge in ignorance,
> Usefulness in harmfulness.
> He does all that one detests.

Epilog-Line 575
(circa 5,000 B.C.E. Ancient Egypt)

The practice of the Precepts should not be thought of as a keeping of rules or somebody else's laws to make your life miserable and dull. You should think of them as your own rules of life which will carry you through the trials of life and guide you to blessedness and peace and true joy. In fact, there is a special excitement that arises when a person discovers that they can control their mind and body and not be a slave to the desires, temptations and pressure from the world.

"Mastery of the passions allows divine thought and action."
—Ancient Egyptian Proverb

Many people learn the ten commandments and then never give them a second thought when they are tempted to commit adultery or steal some object. The mind, weakened by a life of desiring objects and physical pleasure, cannot resist the temptation so it rationalizes what it wants to do even if it knows that action is wrong. You convince yourself that you deserve something (Oh, just this once, who is going to know anyway..) or others should pay for what they did (They have it coming to them), etc. and so the cycle of vice never ends. Why? Because deep down you know what is right and when you act in a way that is contrary to your conscience you develop anger, annoyance and fear. Anger at going against yourself and fear of what the result of your actions will be. These negative emanations are your consequence for going against truth. This consequence is referred to as *Meskent* in Ancient Egyptian philosophy. In Indian Hindu philosophy this concept is referred to as *Karma*. Karma is the result of your actions. It is neither good nor bad in itself. You determine your Karma and this is what the discipline of righteousness is all about. Every untruth is registered in your mind and will haunt you even after death. Therefore, the project is to cleanse the mind of evil intent and then you will be free of evil actions. For if your heart is clear, even if you make mistakes you will not suffer the consequences of evil actions.

Healing the Criminal Heart

All of your actions need to be based on truth. You need to first understand what truth is and then you will know the path of truth. Your daily devotional exercises will provide you with strength to apply the teachings of truth. This is why it is important to pray, chant and meditate on the Divine as prescribed. How many people do you know, who understand that smoking is like suicide and yet they smoke anyway, even if they would like to desperately quit? All the knowledge in the world cannot help you if you lack the will power to implement your knowledge in practice. As Ra is truthful, regular, and harmonious in his heavenly voyage you should seek to be truthful in the three areas of your personality: Your thoughts, your words and your deeds.

Be truthful in your thoughts. From thoughts arise desires and from desires arise actions. Therefore have pure thoughts and your desires and actions will also be pure and will lead you to freedom. Think on the Divine and on the wonder of spiritual freedom which can be yours if you apply yourself to the teachings. When a person is not thinking right they allow the world to get the best of them and this causes anxiety, anger, hatred, fear, etc. For example, if a person calls you a jack-ass will you get upset and say well If I'm a jack ass you are a bigger jack ass or worse? This would be Wrong-thinking because you are not a donkey. On the other hand will you reason that "this person is caught up in the ignorance of the world and how degraded he is that he needs to put me down to feel better about himself.?" This would be Right-thinking. You must remember always that no matter what conditions you may find yourself in you are potentially divine, endowed with the capacity to attain the highest goals of life, as long as you control the lower self. Seek to understand the pain of others an then you will understand your own pain as well as make others understand it. Life is painful only when a person lives in the ignorance which separates them from the ultimate truth. Negative thinking is the worst enemy of every human being. It arises out of ignorance of the truth. This condition is referred to as Delusion.

Be truthful in your words. From words arise negative or positive reactions so do not utter negative words. If you are insulted and you do not reply who is going to fight?

> "If you meet a disputant who is your equal, you will overcome them
> with silence while they speak evilly. Those who witness the encounter
> will remark on this and your name will be held in high esteem among
> the great."
> —Ancient Egyptian "TEACHINGS OF PTAHOTEP"

Be truthful in your deeds. From actions arise consequences. So act righteously and reap the fruits of your actions in the form of good feeling from others, respect, harmony and peace.

> "They who revere *MAAT* are *long lived.*"
> —Ancient Egyptian Proverb

PRINCIPLE TWO: REFLECTIONS ON NON-VIOLENCE

THE PATH OF NON-VIOLENCE

We have explored many dimensions of the theme of non-violence in the precepts of Maat (2, 4, 5, 10 , 12, 14, 23, 25, 29, 33,). Also, the main theme of another wisdom text, the Precepts of Ptahotep, deal with this issue exclusively.

Here the goal is to explore the deeper aspects of non-violence. This can be done by understanding the deep roots of violence and in so doing be able to pull them out of the human personality. As stated earlier, violence arises out of ignorance but how does this ignorance manifest and how does it lead to violence?

> "If you meet a disputant who is more powerful than you, fold your arms and bend your back. Confrontation will not make them agree with you. Disregard their evil speech. Your self control will match their evil utterances and people will call them ignoramuses."
> —Ancient Egyptian "TEACHINGS OF PTAHOTEP"

What is the source of unrighteousness? The source of unrighteousness is ignorance. Ignorance is the force that starts the cycle of vice which leads to all forms of unrighteous desires, thoughts, feelings and actions in all people.

THE CYCLE OF VICE

Violence
↑
Anger and Hatred
↑
Frustration
↑
Negative Actions
↑
Greed, Passion, Weak Will, Irrationality
↑
Desire
↑
IGNORANCE

Consider the teachings which have been presented in Ancient Egyptian Mysticism as well as in all major religions and mystical philosophies from around the world. The central theme is that all life, all existence is indeed part of one whole, one essence, one being. If this is true then everything is related to everything else like a family member. So why is it that people fail to see the connection? It is due to ignorance born of selfish desires, thoughts and feelings. With this understanding the definition of violence must be reinterpreted so that we may understand the heart of the problems of human violence.

Healing the Criminal Heart

The development in spirituality can only occur when a spiritual aspirant allows his or her life to be permeated with truth, justice, correctness, wisdom and righteousness. Righteousness is any activity or movement which leads to self-discovery. Every aspect of life must be placed under the control of the teachings of righteousness, even when the ego is hurt or disappointed by the results. For example, if you enjoy smoking but refrain because deep down you know it is bad for you, then you are living in accordance with truth. Eventually you will discover the greater source of pleasure, health and joy of being in harmony with nature.

The human ego often judges what is good by what pleases it. Therefore, in this way of thinking anything that comes in the way of your desires is considered bad or evil. This feeling leads to anger at what you think is preventing you from getting what will bring pleasure and anger leads to hatred and violence. Feelings and thoughts of anger, hatred and violence constitute a human condition of vice. Vice leads to actions which are disharmonious and these create repercussions which ultimately bring negative results (more anger, hatred and violence) back to the person who originally expressed those feelings and actions. This is the cyclical movement in vice, the *vicious cycle*. Therefore, the wisdom teachings warn against thinking, feeling, acting with vice and associating with those people who are controlled by their vices.

"Go not in and out of court that thy name may not stink."
—Ancient Egyptian Proverb

So one who is practicing virtue must understand that even though an activity may seem pleasurable to the ego it may not be good for promoting a movement in virtue. Examples of this idea abound throughout the Ancient Egyptian Wisdom Texts as you can see by the assortment of proverbs included in this volume. While it may seem good to acquire something by lying, cheating or stealing, in the end, unrighteousness brings pain and sorrow and never fulfillment or contentment. Along with this there is another important point. There is always a witness to a crime. God is the eternal watcher (*Amun*) within every human being, who makes sure that a person never escapes from the repercussions of their actions. This is the Divine law of *Meskhenet (Meskent)* better known in modern times as the law of Karma. Negative occurrences happen in life according to the cycle of vice based on a persons actions (karma). Underlying the cycle of vice is ignorance of the true Self.

Many people feel that once they begin to practice spirituality based on this teaching that they should be spared the past negatives due to the positive in the present. Meskhenet does not work that way. For instance, if you hurt someone ten years ago because you were a negative person then and they held a grudge against you, you cannot expect that they will not still hold anger towards you at present even though you turned to spirituality two years ago. However, in time even these negative repercussions of the past become swept up in the course of time. The most important thing at present is to eradicate the negativity within you which causes the negative feelings, thoughts, words and deeds which lead you to hurt others, and commit various sins against your own conscience. This is what will free you from inner unrest and outward experiences of negativity and adversity. One more important aspect of non-violence is understanding that the entire universe is Divine. The sun, the trees, animals and other human beings are all expressions of the Divine and it is only possible to do violence when this truth is

Healing the Criminal Heart

forgotten. Therefore, remind yourself through your daily practice and remind others as well. Act in kindness and you will develop kindness in your environment.

Many people are disturbed by the violence in the inner city. We know that the gun manufacturers, like the drug dealers, are producing their poison and promoting it with the propaganda that it is a constitutional right and that there are legitimate purposes for having guns. In the cities guns have become the instrument by which people act out their frustrations and hatred. Their easy availability has created a situation in which people can easily act out their violent thoughts and feelings and since the government does not impose the laws of gun control and since the police do not respond to the inner city people are left to their own instinctive animal kill or be killed way of life.

How pathetic it is that people have been driven to accept this hellish way of life on earth when deep down they are all essentially Divine. Will you travel that road of destruction that has been prepared for you by the drug dealers, gun manufacturers and alcohol pushers? Will you accept their desire that you and your family should be subjected to so much violence that you cannot even think of a better life?

You must understand clearly that you may have committed violence but you are not violence. You may have stolen something but you are not thievery. So do not say I am a thief. This would be like saying the God is violence and thievery. You may have committed sins but you are not the sin. So don't say I am a sinner. Say "I am a human being who has acted in a sinful way." Instead say "I am a child of God who has gone astray and acted improperly but now I will fix the error and never allow that to happen again." You may have even killed someone but you are not a killer and no matter how much the world may try to brand you and degrade you and make you feel guilt for the rest of your life you must go beyond this label. Everyone has committed sins, in this life or a past one so everyone is due compassion, forgiveness and redemption when they see the error of their ways. The real you is beyond labels of any kind. First you must realize your mistake and take responsibility. Then you can begin the journey of redemption, forgiveness and amends. Amends means to change for the better, to improve, to remove the faults or errors in your life, to correct your thinking, feeling and actions. When the soul is caught up in such mental delusion, one forgets that one's role (mother, father, boss, employee, etc.) in life is only a vehicle for spiritual discovery, not an end in itself. It is not who you are.

You must realize that the only way that you can be violent is if you are being egoistic. When your mind is full of "I," "me," and "mine," constantly you are developing the pressure of your own selfish identity. So whenever something happens to your body or whenever somebody does something you don't like you ego takes over and spits out angry words, curses and so on. The world is full of ignorant people who believe that the body is the person and nothing more. If you believe in this way you are caught in their web of illusion. You are much more than the ego and you will discover that if you control the ego and purify your mind. Think more of God and your relationship to God instead of so much on yourself and what you want or don't want. Then you will discover that there is something much greater that whatever your ego wants or than whatever anybody else may want. That is the Divine Will of God. When you discover how to follow God's will then you will not have any trouble with the world or with your own ego. This is the blessed state of the Sages.

The Violence of Meat Eating and the Special Food Diet for Followers of Neterian Religion

Chapter 30B of the Ancient Egyptian *Book of Coming Forth By Day* states:

> *This utterance (hekau) shall be recited by a person purified and washed; one who has not eaten animal flesh or fish.*

Plutarch, the ancient Greek historian was an initiate of the temple of Aset (Isis). He reported that the initiates follow a strict vegetarian diet and do not consume alcohol. They study, reflect and meditate on the teachings daily. This an important African legacy which has escaped the view of most historians and African culturalists. Many people are trying to discover their roots and hold on to the features that they find appealing. In reality, ancient African culture bas based on self sacrifice and wisdom and not on the illusion of paradise or isolation. The ancients lived in accordance with the precepts which promote life and not those which promote selfishness and pleasure seeking.

Non-violence also involves vegetarianism. People think that as long as they do not hurt others physically it is OK to say or do or think anything and that its OK to hurt animals and plants. They are life forms and they experience pain and frustration. When they die their pain and anger vibrations enter the food you eat so it is not only poisonous to your intestines and your cells but it is also poisonous to your mind. Studies have proven that meat eating causes increased aggression in meat eaters and aggression pushes the mind away from self-discovery, therefore it is against Maat. If you are in prison, equest the prison authorities that you be provided a vegetarian meal as a part of your religious convictions. Meat is not needed for health. This is a lie put into the media by the meat companies which are managed by greedy people and it is supported by people who are addicted to eating meat. If the United States converted to vegetarianism there would be no hunger anywhere in the world. Protein from almonds is better than protein from beef. Use vitamin supplements to make sure that your physical constitution is up to the challenge of the day. Weakness of the body comes from lack of nutrition, and exercise. Take supplements and perform the basic Yoga exercises each day to the best of your capacity.

PRINCIPLE THREE:
REFLECTIONS ON SELF-CONTROL-RIGHT ACTION
(10, 16, 17, 22, 24, 25, 28, 31, 32, 35, 37, 39)

Self-control was alluded to earlier. You must realize that ultimately you control your destiny. You have brought yourself to your current condition of degradation. But the wonderful news is that you have the means to rise above your present adversity. If you face it with the right attitude you will be stronger and wiser. This is the true reason why God has allowed the calamities to befall you, to bring you to a point where you will see that you are moving away from truth. If you make the necessary adjustments in your life with patience and stick-to-itiveness you will attain positive results, guaranteed!. Now the task is to act in ways that will lead you towards gaining the strength to control your life instead of being a victim of the world. You have the power to control your mind and your body. This is the key.

Self-control will arise in you when you begin to understand the higher goal of life and make up your mind to go after that instead of giving into the pettiness of the world.

First work on controlling your body. Even if you feel like doing something, if you know it is wrong refrain from doing it and then in your prayer time offer your sacrifice to the goddess. She appreciates this more than money, food, incense, etc. True self effort is the highest offering a person can bring to God and it does not have to be in a church or temple but wherever you are.

> The abomination of the soul is too much talking.
> —Ancient Egyptian Proverb.

Next work on controlling your mouth, act as the gatekeeper and do not utter words of untruth or words of truth that will only bring argument and confusion. Do not utter words that promote strife or arguments. Do not say things to make yourself look good in the eyes of others. This will only inflate your ego and lead to trouble later on. Do not talk beyond what is necessary. Too mush talking distracts and agitates the mind. It causes restlessness and delusion. Be introspective and concentrate on whatever you are doing at the time you are doing it. This will help you to practice meditation during your meditation time. If you are loudmouthed and constantly talking you will waste mental energy and you will not be able to think righteously or gain self confidence and will power. The mouth is the portal of the mind and it is a creative instrument. You can create confusion or understanding, the choice is yours.

PRINCIPLE FOUR:
REFLECTIONS ON BALANCE OF MIND-REASON
(13, 19, 26, 30, 36, 38)

> "The heart of the envious is gall and bitterness; his tongue spits venom; the success of his neighbor breaks his rest. He sits in his cell repining; and the good that happens to another, is to him an evil. Hatred and malice feed upon his heart, and there is no rest in him."
> —Ancient Egyptian Proverb

What is balance of mind. Yoga philosophy is an advanced form of psychology and group therapy which is only recently being acknowledged by the established western psychologists. In Yoga science there are four elements to the personality and three major personality types described. The Elements are INTELLECT, EMOTIONS, ACTION and WILL. The Personality types are: DULL, AGITATED, and LUCID. These aspects of the personality must be harmonized in order for a person to discover true peace and contentment. Otherwise a dis-balanced person will be in constant turmoil and distress, constantly seeking, constantly desiring and constantly running after illusion in the world.

THE INTEGRAL YOGA

The personality of every human being is somewhat different from every other. However the Sages of Yoga have identified four basic factors which are common to all human personalities. These factors are: Emotion, Reason (intellect), Action and Will. This means that in order for a human being to evolve, all aspects of the personality must progress in an integral fashion. Therefore, four major forms of Yoga disciplines have evolved and each is specifically designed to promote a positive movement in one of the areas of personality. The Yoga of Devotional Love enhances and harnesses the emotional aspect in a human personality and directs it towards the Higher Self. The Yoga of Wisdom enhances and harnesses the reasoning aspect in a human personality and directs it towards the Higher Self. The Yoga of Action enhances and harnesses the movement and behavior aspect in a human personality and directs it towards the Higher Self. The Yoga of Meditation enhances and harnesses the willing aspect in a human personality and directs it towards the Higher Self.

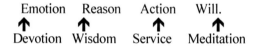

Emotion   Reason   Action   Will.
  ↑   ↑   ↑   ↑
Devotion Wisdom Service Meditation

Thus, Yoga is a discipline of spiritual living which transforms every aspect of personality in an integral fashion, leaving no aspect of a human being behind. This is important because an unbalanced movement will lead to frustration, more ignorance, more distraction and more illusions leading away from the Higher Self. For example, if a person develops the reasoning aspect of personality he or she may come to believe that they have discovered the Higher Self, however when it comes to dealing with some problem of life, such as the death of a loved one, they cannot control their emotions, or if they are tempted to do something unrighteous, such as smoking, they cannot control their actions and have no will power to resist. The vision of Integral Yoga is a lofty goal which every human being can achieve with the proper guidance, self-effort and repeated practice. There is a very simple philosophy behind Integral Yoga. During the course of the day you may find yourself doing various activities. Sometimes you will be quiet, at other times you will be busy at work, at other times you might be interacting with people, etc. Integral Yoga gives you the opportunity to practice yoga at all times. When you have quiet time you can practice meditation, when at work you can practice righteous action and selfless service, when you have leisure time you can study and reflect on the teachings and when you feel the sentiment of love for a person or object you like you can practice remembering the Divine Self who made it possible for you to experience the company of those personalities or the opportunity to acquire those objects. From a higher perspective you can practice reflecting on how the people and objects in creation are expressions of the Divine and this movement will lead you to a spontaneous and perpetual state of ecstasy, peace and bliss which are the hallmarks of spiritual enlightenment. The purpose of Integral Yoga is therefore to promote integration of the whole personality of a human being which will lead to complete spiritual enlightenment. Thus Integral Yoga should be understood as the most effective method to practice mystical spirituality.

The important point to remember is that all aspects of yoga can and should be used in an integral fashion to generate an efficient and harmonized spiritual movement in the practitioner. Therefore, while there may be an area of special emphasis, other elements

Healing the Criminal Heart

are bound to become part of the yoga program as needed. For example, while a yogin may place emphasis on the Yoga of Wisdom, they may also practice Devotional Yoga and Meditation Yoga along with the wisdom studies. Further, it must be understood that as you practice one path of yoga, others will also develop automatically. For example, as you practice the Yoga of Wisdom your faith will increase or as you practice the Yoga of Devotion your wisdom will increase. If this movement does not occur your wisdom alone will by dry intellectualism or your faith alone will be blind faith. So when we speak of wisdom here we are referring to wisdom gained through experience or intuitional wisdom and not intellectual wisdom which is speculative. If you do not practice the teachings through the Yoga of Action, your wisdom and faith will be shallow because you have not experienced the truth of the teachings and allowed yourself the opportunity to test your knowledge and faith. If you do not have introspection and faith, your wisdom and actions you will externalized, agitated and distracted. Your spiritual realization will be insubstantial, weak and lacking stability. You will not be able to meet the challenges of life nor will you be able to discover true spiritual realization in this lifetime or even after death. Therefore, the integral path of yoga, with proper guidance, is the most secure method to achieve genuine spiritual enlightenment. See chart of spiritual paths.

Now we will discuss the three major personality types. For simplicity we will use the analogy of a video cassette player to understand the mind.

The DULL personality is depressed, full of anger, vengefulness, covetousness, hatred, greed, self-destruction, suicidal, meat eater, etc. How did they get this way? They poisoned their mind for so long that the light of the soul barely shines enough to keep them alive. They have entertained thoughts like, "The world is cruel," "I hate life," "I Don't believe in God," "To hell with you and everybody," "If you don't care about me then I don't care about you," and so on. They have desired so many things and have been frustrated so much that they hate the world and themselves so they strike out in the hope of hurting the world and ending their own pain. Their enjoyment is when others are suffering and when they suffer as well. Smoking, drugs and alcohol are forms of suffering and suicide even though they feel good at the time they are used, in reality these are intense forms of pain from a Yogic point of view. In reality they are a call for help because an advanced human being does not have any need for depending on petty things of the world or on objects of drugs to escape the world. A true human being is a master of the world, kings and queens. Anyone else is merely a child from a spiritual point of view. This personality is like a video machine that has stopped playing the movie of life and has begun to chew up the video tape. It has seen so many scenes of violence, hatred, destruction and fear that it has pulled back from life and wants to self destruct. This personality is like a person that cannot even stop and reason that smoking is bad. If you tell them this truth they will even want to fight with you. This is because they are so degraded that the prospect of losing even the poison is unbearable. What does it say about a system that promotes meat and tobacco, knowing that it is purposely addictive and poisonous? The world has unrighteous people who are ready and waiting to exploit others. They are driven by spiritual ignorance, hatred and greed, the same as anyone else. Should you play into their hands and give yourself over as a sacrifice to their greed. They will receive their consequences so do not resent them. Do not be resentful. Resentment leads to negativity and it is therefore against Maat. If you succeed in turning your life around you will deprive them of their desire to exploit you and they will suffer economically and eventually they will have to pay for their own mistakes.

84

Healing the Criminal Heart

"Be free from resentment under the experience of being wronged,"

"Do not conspire against others. GOD will punish accordingly. Schemes do not prevail; only the laws of GOD do. Live in peace, since what GOD gives comes by itself."
—Ancient Egyptian Proverbs

The AGITATED personality is the person who is anxious, with uncontrolled thoughts, unable to calm down, a chain smoker, meat eater, etc. The mind is always racing from one thought to the next, from one scheme to the next and the mind is always full of delusions and haunting memories. They think that they will get over on the world and make the big score, they constantly have to be into something and hate to be alone with their thoughts. This personality is like a video machine that is constantly playing one movie after another. Constant movement and never a moment of introspection. If there is a brief period of introspection the mind is too weak to do what is right. This is like a smoker who knows that smoking is bad but cannot stop himself.

This personality is constantly on a roller-coater of emotions, sometimes joyous and at other times angry or sorrowful. They are constantly elated over some prospect or depressed over some prospect. They anticipate the future, yearning for what they desire and if it does not come they become angry and resentful and frustrated. They have not learned to weather the stormy seas of life's ups and downs and they have no anchor to hold onto. So they are tossed about by the winds and rough seas and they therefore never discover true peace, what the Ancient Egyptians called *HETEP*. They never discover the bliss of the inner self except in brief moments when their pressure is released through sexual activity or in the perception of having gotten what they wanted. How long does the pleasure last when you get something you wanted or after a sexual encounter? Since the disease of agitation is still in the mind, the release of tension is only temporary and the cycle repeats even up to the time of death and beyond. Like a drug addict you must constantly seek that thing you want to fulfill your desires, but you are always frustrated. Most people never discover the reason why and live their lives in constant search. After death their desires push them to more frustrations and so they experience a lesser hell than the DULL personalities but it is still hell nonetheless.

"There is no happiness for the soul in the external worlds since these are perishable, true happiness lies in that which is eternal, within us."
—Ancient Egyptian Proverbs

Therefore, you must realize that the world cannot bring you true peace and fulfillment. Only you can do that. How? By becoming a lucid personality, integrating your personality, keeping the balance of mind. Trust in God and know that all happens for a reason. Know that if you reach for God you will not be disappointed because God is the only truth and never ending reality. God is not here today and then gone tomorrow. God is accessible but only for those who seek. Otherwise you are on your own and you don't stand a chance on your own.

The agitated personality is like that video machine that plays action movies and love story movies, comedy shows, etc. constantly. It is caught up in the emotions of the shows that it play and cries when there is a sad movie and laughs when there is a funny movie and it is always anticipating when it will play the next movie or show. It develops a preference for action movies and hates sad shows and the tape deck has forgotten who he is and he is caught up in the emotions and feelings of the movies. If a sad movie plays he feels sad. If a happy movie plays he is happy. He is confused and never finds true peace and happiness because he is looking for it in the movie and not in realizing who he is, the tape deck which is never really affected by the emotions or actions in the movies that it plays. Every human being's soul is like that tape deck but the constant playing of movies (dramas of human life) has made the soul forget its true nature. This is why yoga prescribes the practice of meditation and devotional worship and reflection on the teachings. These practices help you to remember the truth by giving you a break from the world and the ego desires and activities.

> "See that prosperity elate not thine heart above measure; neither adversity depress thine mind unto the depths, because fortune beareth hard against you. Their smiles are not stable, therefore build not thy confidence upon them; their frowns endure not forever, therefore let hope teach you patience."
>
> —Ancient Egyptian Proverb

The LUCID personality is balanced in pain and in pleasure. He or she knows that the world is a changing arena of ups and downs so therefore there is no reason to fret about life since it is God's will. A good thing it is because if the world was perfect who would seek the Divine? Even though Enlightenment, God, the Kingdom of Heaven, Buddha Consciousness, etc. is a billion times greater that the worldly pleasures of human beings, they would be deluded and they would not care about anything else if there was no adversity in life. Such is the power of sense pleasure which deludes the mind of human beings. For no matter how good your situation is, no matter how many millions, houses, cars, women, etc. you have, it will all end someday and you will feel pain and sorrow.

The answer is to seek that which is not changing, that which is even greater wealth and that which you take with you after death: ENLIGHTENMENT.

> "Consume pure foods and pure thoughts with pure hands, adore celestial beings, become associated with wise ones: sages, saints and prophets; make offerings to GOD."
>
> —FROM THE ANCIENT EGYPTIAN STELE OF TEHUTI-NEFER:

The process of attaining enlightenment involves purifying the mind so as to unburden it from the illusions, delusions and ignorance which act like clouds blocking the sun of Wisdom.

The practical disciplines which leads to lucidity are as follows. According to the teachings of *The Ancient Egyptian Temple Of Aset (Isis)* or the Yoga of Wisdom, the process of Yoga consists of three steps:

1- **Listening** to Wisdom teachings. Having achieved the qualifications of an aspirant, there is a desire to listen to the teachings from a Spiritual Preceptor. There is increasing intellectual understanding of the scriptures and the meaning of truth versus untruth, real versus unreal, temporal versus eternal.

2- **Reflection** on those teachings and living according to the disciplines enjoined by the teachings until the wisdom is fully understood. Reflection implies discovering the oneness behind the multiplicity of the world by engaging in intense inquiry into the nature of one's true Self..

3- **Meditation** The process of reflection leads to a state in which the mind is continuously introspective. It means expansion of consciousness culminating in revelation of and identification with the Absolute Self: God.

The lucid personality is like the video machine from which all movies and shows have been removed. It is sitting there idle, just waiting to see what will happen next but not anticipating a new movie or regretting the absence of a movie. It knows it is a tape player only and separate from the movies. It is free from its delusion of thinking that it is feeling what the movies are playing within him. This is the pure state of mind.

PRINCIPLE FIVE:
REFLECTIONS ON: NOT-STEALING
(3, 6, 7, 9, 40, 41, 42)

What is stealing? Many people think that stealing is when you pilfer the possessions of others. This is only the gross form of stealing. Stealing begins in the mind and it has many different stages. It begins with negative desires and these lead to craving for what you desire. The cravings lead to negative thoughts and these lead to negative actions, stealing. "I want to experience pleasure." "I like that car." These are desires. "I must have pleasure." "I must have that car!" These are cravings. "Who does he think he is? I deserve that and he got it without even working for it! I'm of this race and that makes me better so it is my right to take his stuff!" These are negative thoughts. When the pressure of negative desiring and thinking reaches a peak, people act out and disregard reason or the consequences and then they experience the backlash for what they have done. A really deluded person might even blame the victim for the crime. A thief may say to a police officer who just caught him, Its his (the victim's) fault. He has so many things and I have wanted the car." This is of course perverted and twisted logic and those who have twisted thinking will come to no good.

These kinds of thoughts are poison to the mind and since your deeper self rejects these egoistic thoughts a person deep down feels pain even though on the surface they seem to be arrogant, violent and vulgar. Everyone wants the same thing peace and joy. But being beset with ignorance, and having not received proper guidance in the ways of virtuous living, people have learned from television, politicians, community leaders, the movies and their peers that it is alright to desire even the things that are necessary for life. Also, people learn that it is OK to commit crimes as long as you don't get caught or as long as you have enough money to get off. Then when a person sees injustices, how some keep better jobs and exclude others or how some people do not care for others, they become bitter and resentful.

You have the power to lead your mind to understand the glory of God or you can lead your mind to greater Agitation and Dullness. It is your choice. All injustice that exists is there for the purpose of showing you the righteous way. Will you learn the lesson or will you suffer more? The fact that you have read this book shows your inclination towards peace and enlightenment. Do not pass up this opportunity. There is so much at stake for your future.

> "Gods are immortal men, and men are mortal Gods."
> —Ancient Egyptian Proverb

Whenever you think about stealing you have already committed a sin against yourself. You are deep down united with God. Your idea of stealing is like saying "I am a miserable personality and I need this cigarette, or this TV set or this car to make me happy." You are turning away from your own greatness and lowering yourself to a place below snakes. The yogic definition of sin must be explained. Sin is anything that takes you away from the knowledge of the Self. It is a deviation from truth which leads the soul astray. It is not to be understood in the way espoused by the Orthodox Churches, as a blot on your soul which cannot be erased ever. This is not the original meaning intended by Jesus or Muhammad or any great religious leader. Sin is a mistake due to ignorance. When ignorance is removed all since are also removed. Therefore, a person can have the possibility of redemption. Otherwise there would be no way out and no purpose for you to engage in any spiritual studies or practices at all.

> "Do not plunder your neighbor's house or steal the goods of one that is
> near you, lest they denounce you before you are even heard."
> —Ancient Egyptian Proverb

Depriving others of their rightful possessions in any way, shape or form is stealing. If you are a doctor and you tell a patient to have an operation they don't need you are a thief. If you are a mechanic and you tell a woman to replace parts that she does not need you are a thief and you have committed sin. If you are a sales person and you sell items that people don't need, just to get rich you are a thief and you have committed sin, even if the laws allow you to do what you have done. The law of the land can be as corrupt as the business people and the politicians. You are the higher court which determines guilt or innocence in your own trial of life. God does not judge you. God only helps you to go to the place where you have led yourself (Hell or Heaven). Hell and heaven are experienced while on earth as well as after death. Therefore, learn the Precepts of Maat well and then you will have a good guide for what is righteous and what is unrighteous.

When you hoard wealth that you don't need and you have deprived others of things they need you have committed sin. If you keep others in poverty as you get rich you are a thief and you will bring on yourself adversity in your personal life and you will never have peace no matter how much you have. You will judge yourself at the time of death by the actions of your life and you will experience pain you have brought to others in the form of your own frustration and sorrow at losing your true self in the illusions of the world.

PRINCIPLE SIX:
REFLECTIONS ON SEX-SUBLIMATION
(11, 20, 21)

What is sexuality? Sexuality is seeing yourself as a sexual being instead of as a human being. More instruction on this point comes from the Ancient Egyptian Bible with Aset's teaching to Heru:

> 125 "Souls, Horus, son, are of the self same nature in themselves, in that they are from one and the same place where the Creator modeled them; nor male nor female are they. Sex is a thing of bodies, not of souls."

The soul has no sex but since it desires to come into the world it must do so as one gender or the other. This is because all creation exists in the form of a duality, opposites such as male-female, hot-cold, dry-wet, heavy-light, etc. This is so because otherwise there could be no human experience. Why? Because human experience is relative. You must have an opposite or else you cannot know one object from another. Up cannot exist without down and male cannot exist without female.

The real purpose of sexuality is to perpetuate life so that the Self may have human experience. However, this does not mean the indiscriminate incarnation of souls. Like all else this process needs to be governed by Maat. The problems of overpopulation and disorder in society dictate that indiscriminate childbearing is against Maat in this time and history. Also, the ancient texts and modern science show that promiscuity debilitates a person both physically and mentally. This causes a weakness in reasoning and the ability to create ideas and to resolve problems. Therefore, promiscuity is against Maat. When people bring children into the world before they are ready to deal with them children become a great burden both financially and as a source of stress. Therefore, bringing children into the world before you are ready is against Maat. If you bring children into the world and do not take care of them you are turning away from your karmic duty to the child and you will have to deal with the repercussions if you do not try to make amends for your actions.

"Be circumspect in matters of sexual relations."
—Ancient Egyptian Proverb

Society has come to believe that sexuality is for pleasure and fun or domination and denigration of others. Sexual desire is more than a means for physical gratification. All your desires are sexual desires because the objective of sex is to unite with something. When you have sex relations, deep down you are trying to bond with that someone but since you cannot, except in the illusion of a momentary orgasm. Instead of fulfillment you become frustrated and mentally weakened. Sex then becomes a means to relieve stress and like a drug it flares up more desire and no brings no fulfillment.

Children are often used in the same way. A person may bring them into the world with the idea of having someone to love but the idea degenerates into a burden when the reality of dealing with a new person's ego (the child) emerges. In the degraded state a person may hate their own children, wife, parents, etc. and even kill them, all due to frustrated desire. Overindulgence in desire renders the mind dull and in that state a person is the worst kind of slave to the world.

Healing the Criminal Heart

Relationships are the way in which a person learns how to grow in love by caring for someone other than your little self, the I me and mine which we discussed earlier. This is a positive process if it happens when your ready. So if you have a wife or husband at the proper time in your life, when you have matured to realize that person is not an object for your pleasure, and when you realize that they cannot make you happy but that your relationship can help you to work out the mysteries of life, then you can marry. When you understand that you do not own your spouse and when you begin to act selflessly for their sake instead of your own and when you are both established in the respect for each other and in worship of the Divine, then you will be ready to make the decision about bringing a child into the world or not. You must realize that you do not create anything in this world. God creates everything through you. Therefore, you should turn away from the egoistic ideas of creating a child and how some child belongs to you and you should give up the idea of egoistic pride in your children. Then you will be able to see them for who they are and you will be able to love them and all children as souls full of the spirit of God. If you choose to you should bring no more than one child into the world. A better choice for our time is adoption. In your new universal vision you should start to see that all children are your children. So it should not matter if they came from your body or not. This is the highest practice of spirituality in household life. In Ancient Egypt there were priests and priestesses who were married and who had children and there were those who remained celibate and dedicated themselves to the service of the temple exclusively. If you choose to have children you must rear them in the spiritual path and as you do this you will also grow because in order to teach them you must be the example. Otherwise your teachings will fall on deaf ears. As you become the example you will purify yourself and show them the way to blessedness by following in your footsteps.

> " If your child accepts your words then no plan of theirs will go wrong. So teach your son to be a hearer, one who will be valued by the officials, one who will guide their speech by what they have been told, one who is regarded as a hearer. The children will reach old age if they listen to the wise words of their parents."
> —Ancient Egyptian Proverb

A healthy sexual relationship and a healthy family are not based on pleasure or selfishness but on sacrifice. You cannot unite with anyone sexually in a physical sense but if you control your desire and channel it into discovering God within yourself and that other person you can unite in your souls. Therefore, infidelity, lust, being a player, etc. are in reality forms of intense illusion into which the Agitated and Dull witted minded people have fallen.

The soul incarnates as a male for the purpose of growing in reason since the male physiology is more conducive to reasoning. Also, a soul may incarnate as a male if it has experienced desire and fixation on the male personality in a previous lifetime. A soul may incarnate as a female personality to work out emotional issues since the female constitution is conducive to processing emotions more than the male. It is important to understand that if you hurt the opposite sex you are bound to incarnate as that gender in your next life and you will find yourself in a relationship where you will experience the same hurt you have perpetrated. In this manner, the process of reincarnation teaches the soul and eventually, after thousands of incarnations, a person may learn to be truthful and honest. This is the long and painful way to spiritual evolution.

If you apply yourself and follow the teaching presented here, you will make up for your past misdeeds and create a new destiny of light instead of darkness. The fact that you are reading this indicates that your soul has led you, through a mysterious process, to a person or a situation which has caused this book to come into your possession. Now that you know these truths you are more responsible than before for your actions because now you have an intensified awareness of the consequences of actions. Therefore, resolve to make amends for the past and look to a renewed future of joy and peace and prosperity.

Forgiveness is the first step towards redemption. First forgive yourself for sinning against yourself and then seek the forgiveness of those whom you have hurt and resolve to eradicate the cause of your negative actions. Otherwise no amount of forgiveness or penance will help you. You must get to the source of unrighteousness: IGNORANCE OF THE KNOWLEDGE OF YOUR TRUE DIVINE SELF.

One other important form of ignorance which leads many people astray in their idea about sex is that it proves one's manhood or womanhood. People are deluded by their lack of understanding the meaning of life. So they seek what society tells them that they should seek, a mate, children, money, youth, fame, etc. But none of these will help you to be happy unless you acquire them by actions performed with Maat. Anything you get into for unrighteous reasons will become an adversity, even if it seems easy and appears to bring you lots of pleasure in the beginning. You are more than the body. Animals can have offspring. How are you different from them? Many people are worse than animals because at least animals take care of their young. Many parents do not. If you cannot afford children do not have them. When you discover your true identity, your higher self, you will grow beyond the childish need to prove your manhood or womanhood as a childbearing machine. The teenage pregnancies only serve to bring more misery, confusion and heartache to people's lives. The child prevents them from achieving higher goals and degrades them because they cannot take care of it properly so they feel bad an depressed inside. Will you allow this pattern to continue in your life? Become a positive force in the world by changing your life and thereby becoming an example for others and be part of the revolution of righteousness which I is long overdue in our times.

Parenting or Spiritual Partnership

"Those who hath learned to know themselves, hath reached that Good which does transcend abundance; but they who through a love that leads astray, expend their love upon their body; they stay in Darkness wandering, and suffering through their senses things of Death."

Ancient Egyptian Proverb

Many times parents fall into the trap of attachment (*they who through a love that leads astray*) and egoistic desires in relation to their children. Your child does not, never will and never has belonged to you. So why treat them as possessions? Why bring them into the world only so that you can have someone to love or so that you

91

can feel that you are having progeny and a legacy, or so that you can be proud of your virility or fertility or so that you can boast of their achievements which you were unable to accomplish, etc. These are all egoistic notions based on your own egoistic desires. At a higher level of spiritual experience you can discover that you are related to all children of the universe. This is what a Sage, a person who has matured in spirituality, experiences and this is why they do not feel the need to procreate in an ordinary manner. Rather, they discover that they can create wondrous works of spiritual literature and that they can affect the hearts of thousands of people with their mere presence when they have reached a certain state of spiritual purification.

Many people in modern society have developed the idea that it is good to depend on others as sources of happiness. They think it proper to live vicariously through their children. They see their own lives as unfulfilling and sometimes even as failures so they strive to push their children to succeed according to societies standards of success (money, fame, status, progeny, etc.) without understanding that these values are what led them (the parents) to the state in which they presently find themselves. But does this make any sense? Is it a good idea to place ones hopes on others who are subject to the whims of their own mentality as well as the unpredictability of life? You need to develop higher ideals for yourself which will lead you to discover your own purpose and your own fulfillment. When this occurs you will become a real source of wealth for the world and for your family. As a parent on the spiritual path you need to discover the joy of not depending on your child as a source of pleasure, pride or sentimental attachment. As you develop this quality of detachment from egoism and attachment to the spiritual essence of the heart you will be able to pass it on to your child. In so doing you will both develop a deeper form of love which goes beyond the superficial attachments which most people consider as the norm.

If you choose married life and the path of parenthood and want to also practice mystical spirituality this is possible if you see your life as a parent and your life as a wife or husband as a means to gathering the experiences which will help you to grow spiritually. This means that you will seek these relationships with people who will have the same goal and you will serve your family as you would serve humanity, selflessly and righteously without egoistic attachment and sentimentality based on ignorance and personal desires for sex or to be looked up to and admired as a producer of children as a breeding mare or bull.

Many times people misunderstand love with attachment and the prospect of fulfilling their own personal desires through their relationships. In so doing they lose the opportunity to build a strong and lasting relationship because egoistic desires can never be satisfied with an object or condition in the world of time and space. The human mind is in reality desiring something much higher than anything it can get from the world. This is why when relationships which are based on superficiality lose their novelty, passion or excitement people who fell in love with each other based on the egoistic ideals are eager to separate and move on in the search for more excitement. However, since they have not repaired the errors of their way of egoism they will only produce the same conditions with the next partner they encounter.* Since no partner can keep them excited all the time they will never discover true

Healing the Criminal Heart

fulfillment or peace in their life and they will die as disappointed personalities. *(See *Egyptian Tantra Yoga: The Art of Sex Sublimation and Universal Consciousness*).

"Through firm instruction one can master one's emotions"

Ancient Egyptian Proverb

As a spiritual aspirant you must be perfectly clear on one point. You will never discover the higher levels of spiritual enlightenment if you hold on to egoistic attachments and desires be they related to objects or conditions of the world or to family members including your child. This also relates to the practice of spirituality. If you hold onto elementary teachings you will not be able to progress to more advanced teachings. Therefore, your vision must be higher than that of an ordinary parent. You must keep the prospective of growing to discover and see yourself and your child as spiritual beings and not as relations. In a higher sense you are both God's children so to speak and from an even higher perspective you are not related as parent and child but as the self same nature, the Divine. This also applies to your spouse and to every other human being on earth. The deepest reality is that you are related beyond any undoing. No distance, worldly condition or even death can untie the bonds between souls and between souls and God. Therefore, a new vision must emerge in the heart based on spiritual truth rather than egoistic sentiment.

In fact you must learn to be prepared to let them go at any time without feeling resentment or grief. In human life death can come at any time due to disease or accidents or other causes. Therefore, is it wise to hold something dear which can be taken away at a moments notice? Rather, you should learn to love your child's eternal and immortal essence, that which is imperishable and cannot be destroyed, the Divine essence within them. Also, you should learn to trust God who is working through nature, to lead them to the situations and circumstances they need to grow spiritually without resentment over something than may appear as bad or as good. People place these values on things but God sees them as good to the extent that they lead a human being towards spiritual evolution. To this end evil as well as good are only the means used to lead the soul towards self-discovery. In this manner you can also learn to forgive your child when they commit errors due to ignorance and egoism since you realize that it is ignorance operating and not the Divine Self within. Learn to accept the movements of nature as God's plan even while you strive to work towards bettering your life in all regards, spiritual and financial. Learn to develop detachment towards the feelings of selfishness and greed and don't seek to acquire more than is necessary for your needs. You will find that you will discover inner peace and contentment which will allow you to enter into greater and greater awareness of the spiritual reality which is all around you. As you become more and more spiritually aware your child will be exposed to your radiation of wisdom and courage. This inner spiritual strength will be a formidable force against the negativity of the outside world. You should encourage your child to cherish life as a precious gift from God but not in a sentimental way based on attachment and egoistic desires.

The mastery over one's emotions and desires is the cornerstone of spiritual realization. This exalted attainment is certainly possible. Very few people in history have discovered the joy of reaching a desireless state wherein there is no tension or anxiety over what one wants, what one strives to hold onto or cannot get. Great Sages throughout history have discovered this and they left their legacy in the form of the mystical religions and yoga philosophies from around the world for all peoples. Therefore, realize that you, as well as your child, have the potential to become great sages since the great figures of history were no different from you or your child. The difference is that they undertook the study and practice of the mystical teachings. So begin today to follow the royal road to spiritual enlightenment.

PART III: The Daily Schedule for Spiritual Practice

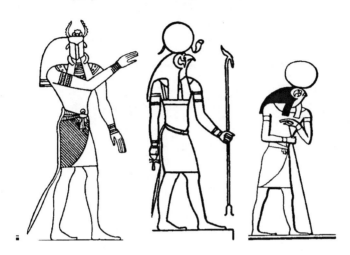

The three forms of Ra: Khepra, Ra and Tem.
(Morning, Noon and Dusk – i.e. The Beginning, The Middle and The End of Creation. =
God is All-Encompassing Divinity)

A practitioner of Yoga must be able to integrate the main practices of yoga into daily life. This means that you need to begin adding small amounts of time for Prayer, Repetition of the Divine Name (Hekau), Exercise (includes proper breathing exercise), Study of the Teachings, Silence, Selfless Service, Meditation, and Daily Reflection. This also means that you will gradually reduce the practices which go against yogic movement as you gain more time for Shedi.

Below you will find an outline of a schedule for the beginning practice of Yoga. The times given here are a suggested minimum time for beginners. You may spend more time according to your capacity and personal situation, however, try to be consistent in the amount of time and location you choose to practice your discipline as well as in the time of day you choose to perform each of the different practices. This will enable your body and mind to develop a rhythm which will develop into the driving force of your day. When this occurs you will develop stamina and fortitude when dealing with any situation of life. You will have a stable center which will anchor you to a higher purpose in life whether you are experiencing prosperous times or adverse times. In the advanced stages, spiritual practice will become continuous. Try to do the best you can according to your capacity, meaning your circumstances. As you develop, you may feel drawn toward some forms of practice over others. The important thing to remember is to practice them all in an integrated fashion. Do not neglect any of the practices even though you may spend additional time on some versus others.

Practicing spirituality only during times of adversity is the mistake of those who are spiritually immature. Any form of spiritual practice, ritualistic or otherwise is a positive development, however, you will not derive the optimal spiritual benefits by simply becoming religious when you are in trouble. The masses of people only pray when they are in trouble...then they ask for assistance to get out of trouble. What they do not realize is that if they were to turn their minds to God at all times, not just in times of misfortune, adversity would not befall them. As you progress through your studies you will learn that adversities in life are meant to turn you toward the Divine. In this sense they are messages from the Divine to awaken spiritual aspiration. However, if you do not listen to the message and hearken to the Divine intent behind it, you will be in a position to experience more miseries of life and miseries of a more intense nature.

Basic Schedule of Spiritual Practice

The following prayers should be uttered in the morning, noon and evening daily. Some of the terms will be foreign to you in the beginning. However, as you study the teachings the deeper meanings will open up to you. For now you must focus on the affirmations of Maat (Righteousness) which are contained within the prayers. Following the prayers practice chanting followed by meditation as instructed in the chanting and meditation sections. Sit in a comfortable posture on a chair or cross-legged on the ground

Morning Worship: Ushet In The Morning (Facing the eastern Horizon)

Hymn to Khepera as Neberdjer:

"Neb-er-djer saith, I am the creator of what hath come into being, and I myself came into being under the form of the god Khepera, and I came into being in primeval time. I had union with my hand, and I embraced my shadow in a love embrace; I poured seed into my own mouth, and I sent forth from myself issue in the form of the gods Shu and Tefnut." "I came into being in the form of Khepera, and I was the creator of what came into being, I formed myself out of the primeval matter, and I formed myself in the primeval matter. My name is Asar.

 *Neb-er-tcher (Neberdjer)*

Neberdjer Speaks:
I was alone, for the gods and goddesses were not yet born, and I had emitted from myself neither Shu nor Tefnut. I brought into my own mouth, *hekau* (the divine words of power), and I forthwith came into being under the form of things which were created under the form of Khepera."

Prayer to Amun:

O Åmen, O Åmen, who art in heaven, turn thy face upon the dead body of the child, and make your child sound and strong in the Underworld.

O Åmen, O Åmen, O God, O God, O Åmen, I adore thy name, grant thou to me that I may understand thee; Grant thou that I may have peace in the Tuat, and that I may possess all my members therein...

Hail, Åmen, let me make supplication unto thee, for I know thy name, and thy transformations are in my mouth, and thy skin is before my eyes. Come, I pray thee, and place thou thine heir and thine image, myself, in the everlasting underworld... let my whole body become like that of a neter, let me escape from the evil chamber and let me not be imprisoned therein; for I worship thy name..

NEXT: Repetition of the Divine Name – Choose a Hekau and chant for 10 minutes

NEXT: Meditation practice (10 minutes in Am, should be practiced after exercise, prayer and repetition of the Divine Name)

Closing Prayer after meditation or any spiritual practice:

I am pure. I am pure. I am Pure.
I have washed my front parts with the waters of libations, I have cleansed my hinder parts with drugs which make wholly clean, and my inward parts have been washed in the liquor of Maat.

NOON Worship: Ushet In The MIDDAY (Facing the north)

—from the Ancient Egyptian *Book of Coming Forth By Day* (Translated by Muata Ashby – see the book of the Dead by Muata Ashby for details and Gloss)

THE LITANY TO THE SUN

Adorations to Ra when He rises in the Eastern Horizon of Heaven.

1. Behold Asar_____ bringing divine offerings of all the gods and goddesses. Asar _____ speaks thus:

2. Homage to thee, who comes in the form of Khepri (Morning sun, solar child-Nefertem.), Khepri the Creator of the gods and goddesses. You rise and shine, illuminating your mother, goddess Nut, the sky, crowned as king of the gods and goddesses. Your mother Nut worships you with her two arms. The western horizon receives you in peace and Maat embraces you at the double season. Give Asar _____ Glorious Spirit being, (i.e. allow the initiate to become an Akhu or Glorious Spirit.) and spiritual strength through righteous speaking. Grant the ability to come forth as a living soul so that Asar _____ may see Heru of the two Horizons. (The All-Encompassing Divine Self in the form of Heru.) Grant this to the Ka (Spiritual essence of the personality which holds a person's desires, impulses and impetus to incarnate; the Life Force which sustains the physical being.) of Asar _____ who is Righteous of Speech in the presence of Asar, the Divine Self. Asar _____ says: Hail to all the gods and goddesses, weighers of the house of the soul, in heaven and on earth by means of the scales of Maat, who are givers of Life Force sustenance.

3. Tatunen, (Creator -aspect of Ra, Atum, Asar, Khepri, Amun, Neberdjer, etc) who first arose on the primeval mound. Protector of the souls of Asar and Heru.) One, maker of men and women as well as the company of the gods and goddesses of the south, the north, the west and the east, i.e. all the neteru, (Gods and goddesses) grant praises to Ra, the lord of heaven, sovereign of life, vitality and health, maker of the gods and goddesses. Adorations to thee in your form as all goodness, as you rise in your boat. The beings up high praise thee. Beings in the lower realms praise thee. Djehuti (Ibis headed deity, minister of Ra, originator of hieroglyphic writings and music.) and Maat (Goddess of righteousness, truth, regularity, and order.) have written for thee, who are shining forth, every day. Your enemies are put to the fire. The fiends are put down, their arms and legs being bound securely for Ra. The children of weakness disrespect and insurrection shall not continue.

4. The great house (Royal family.) is in festival time. The voices of the participants are in the great temple. The gods and goddesses are rejoicing. They see Ra in his glorious rising, his beams of light piercing, inundating the lands. This exalted and venerable god journeys on and unites with the land of Manu, the western horizon,

99

illuminating the land of his birth every day and at the same time he reaches the province where he was yesterday.

5.   Be in peace with me! I see your beauties and I prosper upon the land; I smile and I defeat the ass fiend as well as the other fiends. Grant that I may defeat Apep (Leader of the fiends, second only to Set.) in his time of strength and to see the pilot fish of the Divine Boat of Ra, which is in its blessed pool. (The pool or lake is the symbol of the Primeval Ocean. In ancient times the temple complexes included a lake for ritually sailing the boat of Ra as well as for keeping fish, crocodiles and other animals as temple mascots.) I see Heru in the form as the guardian of the rudder. Djehuti and Maat are upon his two arms. Received am I in the prow (Front section of a ship's hull, the bow.) of the Mandet (The name of Ra's Divine boat when it is traveling from noon to midnight, i.e. the evening boat.) Boat and in the stern of the Mesektet (The name of Ra's Divine boat when it is traveling from midnight to noon, i.e. the morning boat.) Boat. Ra gives divine sight, to see the Aten, (The sundisk.) view the moon god unceasingly, every day, and the ability of souls to come forth, to walk to every place they may desire. Proclaim my name! Find him in the wood board of offerings. There have been given to me offerings in the life-giving presence, like it is given to the followers of Heru. (In Kemetic Mystical Philosophy the principle of "Shemsu Heru" is very important. It may be likened to the disciples of Jesus in Christianity who were his "followers." It means living and acting like Heru, a life of truth and increasing spiritual enlightenment.) is done for me in the divine place in the boat on the day of the sailing, the journey of The God. I am received in the presence of Asar in the land of truth speaking (maakheru) of the Ka of Asar _____.

NEXT: Repetition of the Divine Name – Choose a Hekau and chant for 10 minutes

NEXT: Meditation practice (10 minutes in Am, should be practiced after exercise, prayer and repetition of the Divine Name)

Closing Prayer after meditation or any spiritual practice:

I am pure. I am pure. I am Pure.
I have washed my front parts with the waters of libations, I have cleansed my
hinder parts with drugs which make wholly clean, and my inward parts have
been washed in the liquor of Maat.

Evening Worship: Ushet In The Evening (Facing the Western Horizon)

The following is a Hymn to the Supreme Being in the form of Tem or the setting sun. In the theology surrounding the god Ra, Ra is seen as a representation of the Supreme Being (Neberdjer, Pa Neter). As such Ra is depicted as the sun and the sun has three phases which it manifests every day. These phases are the morning, the middle of the day and the setting sun. Thus we have the following quotation:

In the Myth of Ra and Aset Ra says, "I am Khepera in the morning, and Ra at noonday, and Temu in the evening.

Thus, the following hymn is effective for the evening hours, prior to practicing intense meditation and also at the time of death. In the mystical mythology of the ancient Egyptian city of Anu (Sun city) it is understood that Ra travels in barque which is itself the sun. From this barque hang cords by which those who are righteous can grab hold of in order to be lifted unto the boat. Thus through the practice of Maat (righteous living) one is able to be raised to the company of Ra who travels on the boat of millions of years (eternity) and thus attain immortality and communion with God. For more on this teaching see the books *Resurrecting Osiris* and The Mystical Teachings of The Ausarian Resurrection: Initiation Into the Third Level of Shetaut Asar.

A HYMN TO RA-TEM
(From the papyrus of Lady Mut Hetep)

The lady Mut-Hetep says, "0 Ra-Tem, in thy splendid progress thou risest, and thou settest as a living being "in the glories of the western horizon; thou settest in thy "territory which is in the Mount of Sunset (Manu). "Thy Uraeus is behind thee, thy Uraeus is behind thee. Homage (Ushet) to thee, 0 thou -who art in peace; homage to thee, 0 thou who art in peace. Thou art joined unto the Eye of Tem, and it chooseth its powers of protection [to place] behind thy members. Thou goest forth through heaven, thou travellest over the earth, and thou journeyest onward. 0 Luminary, the northern and southern halves of heaven come to thee, and they bow low in adoration, and they do homage unto thee, day by day. The gods of Amentet rejoice in thy beauties, and the unseen places sing hymns of praise unto thee. Those who dwell in the Sektet boat go round about thee, and the Souls of the East do homage "to thee, and when they meet thy Majesty they cry: "Come, come in peace!" There is a shout of welcome to thee, 0 lord of heaven and governor of Amentet! Thou art acknowledged by Aset (Isis) who seeth her son ,Heru (Horus) in thee, the lord of fear, the mighty one of terror. Thou settest as a living being in the hidden place. Thy father [Ta-]tunen raseth thee up and he placeth both his hands behind thee; thou becomest endowed with divine attributes in [thy] members of earth; thou wakest in peace and thou settest in Manu. Grant thou that I may become a being honoured before Asar (Osiris), and that I may come to thee, 0 Ra-Tem! I have adored thee, therefore do thou for me that which I wish. Grant thou that I may be victorious in the presence of the company of the gods. Thou art beautiful, 0 Ra, in thy western horizon of Amentet, thou lord of Maat, thou being who art greatly feared, and whose attributes are majestic, 0 thou who art greatly beloved by those who dwell in the Tuat! Thou shinest with thy beams upon the beings that are therein perpetually, and thou sendest forth thy light upon the path of Ra-stau. Thou openest up the path of the double Lion-god (Aker), thou settest the gods upon [their] thrones, and the spirits in their abiding places. The heart of Naarerf (i.e., An-rut-f, a region of the Underworld) is glad [when] Ra setteth; the heart of Nahrerf is glad when Ra setteth. Hail, 0 ye gods of the land of Amentet who make offerings and oblations unto Ra-Tem, ascribe ye glory [unto him when] ye meet him. Grasp ye your weapons and overthrow ye the fiend Seba on behalf of Ra, and repulse the fiend Nebt on behalf of Asar. The gods of the land of Amentet rejoice and lay hold upon the cords of the Sektet boat, and they come in peace; the gods of the hidden place who dwell in Amentet triumph.

NEXT: Repetition of the Divine Name – Choose a Hekau and chant for 10 minutes

NEXT: Meditation practice (10 minutes in Am, should be practiced after exercise, prayer and repetition of the Divine Name)

Closing Prayer after meditation or any spiritual practice:

I am pure. I am pure. I am Pure.
I have washed my front parts with the waters of libations, I have cleansed my
hinder parts with drugs which make wholly clean, and my inward parts have
been washed in the liquor of Maat.

Add the following practices as your time allows:

1-Study of the teachings (reading 30 minutes per day),
2-Silence time (30 minutes per day),
3-Selfless service (as required whenever the opportunity presents itself),
4-Daily reflection: Remembering the teachings during the ordinary course of the day and applying them in daily living situations- to be practiced as much as possible.

The suggested times given above are the minimum amount you should spend on daily spiritual practices each day. Whenever possible you should increase the times according to your capacity and ability. You should train your mind so that it rejoices in hearing about and practicing the teachings of yoga instead of the useless worldly activities. Follow this path gradually but steadily.

Once you have established a schedule of minimal time to devote to practices, even if you do 5-10 minutes of meditation time per day and nothing else, keep your schedule if at all possible. Many people feel that they do not have the time to incorporate even ordinary activities into their lives. They feel overwhelmed with life and feel they have no control. If there is no control it is because there is no discipline. If you make a schedule for all of your activities (spiritual and non-spiritual) and keep to it tenaciously, you will discover that you can control your time and your life. As you discover the glory of spiritual practice, you will find even more time to expand your spiritual program. Ultimately, you will create a lifestyle which is entirely spiritualized. This means that every act in your life will be based on the wisdom teachings (MAAT) and therefore you will not only spend a particular time of day devoted to spiritual practices, but every facet of your life will become a spontaneous worship of the divine.

EXERCISE:

Physical postures and exercises were an integral part of the spiritual process in ancient Egypt. The gods and goddesses are depicted in poses which are almost identical to the poses of Indian Hatha Yoga. Yoga exercises are excellent for maintaining flexibility and strength of the body. When the muscles are tightened and flexed they secure the structure, making it work more efficient and stemming the process of deterioration while flushing out impurities as they massage the internal organs. The Qi Gong system of China has similar exercises known as Wei Dan Qi. In addition, because these exercises emphasize focusing on the breath, they draw one's consciousness internally. This internalization of one's consciousness is a necessary prerequisite for meditation, so these exercises are recommended prior to the practice of formal meditation. Thus, they are termed "psycho-physical" and "psycho-spiritual" exercises.

Exercise is also helpful in controlling the emotions. Depression, negativity and agitation in the mind are characterized by a sedentary nature. Therefore, do not allow yourself to become lethargic, apathetic, listless, or uninterested, especially in times of adversity or depression. Keep to your spiritual program in bad times as well as the good. Yoga and Tai Chi exercises are designed to have a special psycho-physical effect which releases energy blocks and develops positive flow of energy which in turn affects the mind in a positive way. The idea is to break the pattern of your established mental and emotional self and to introduce a new pattern that is directed toward peace and inner development.

Meditation In Life

Meditation is not just an exercise that is to be practiced only at a certain time or at a certain place. In order for your meditative efforts to be successful, the philosophy of meditation must become an integral part of your life. This means that the meditative way of life, the yoga lifestyle, must become the focus of your life no matter what else is going on in your life. Most people who do not practice yoga cannot control the clamoring thoughts of the mind and because of this, do not experience inner peace or clarity of purpose in life. Others, beset by intensely negative thoughts, succumb to these and commit acts against their conscience and suffer the consequences of a self-defeating way of life wherein painful situations and disappointments in life are increased while happiness and contentment are decreased. The mind is weakened due to the mental energy being wasted in useless endeavors which only serve to further entangle one in complex relationships and commitments. Another source of weakening one's will to act correctly to promote situations of advancement and happiness is caused by the susceptibility to negative emotions. Negative emotions such as anger, hatred, greed, gloom, sorrow, and depression as well as excessive positive emotions such as elation serve to create mental agitation and desire which in turn cloud the intellectual capacity to make correct decisions in life.

> "Virtues fail that are frustrated by passion at every turn."
> —Ancient Egyptian Proverb

When life seems unbearable due to the intensification of negative emotions and the obscuring of intellectual capacity, some people commit suicide in an attempt to escape or end the painful onslaught of uncontrollable thoughts. Still others prefer to ignore the messages from the deeper Self which are beckoning them to move toward introspection.

Healing the Criminal Heart

Situations of stress in life are motivators whose purpose is to turn us away from the outer world because we have lost our balance. There is a place for material wealth and sensual experience (outer experiences of the senses), however, when the inner reality is ignored or when inner needs and inner development is impaired due to excess concentration on worldly goals and desires, then experiences of frustration and disappointment occur. If these situations are understood as messages from nature to pull back and find the inner balance, then personality integration and harmony can be discovered. However, if these times are faced with lack of inner strength, then they lead to suffering. Sometimes there are moments of clarity wherein the Higher Self is perceived in an intuitive flash but people usually tend to discount the occurrence as a coincidence or other curious event while others in bewilderment believe they are going mad. Others prefer to ignore the issue of spirituality altogether and simply shun any thoughts about death or the afterlife. This is a reverse-yogic movement that stunts spiritual evolution. Its root-cause is fear of the unknown and fear of letting go. The practice of yogic meditation techniques can serve to counteract any and all negative developments in the mind if the correct techniques are used and the correct understanding is adopted.

There are four main components of meditation. These are: posture, breath-life force control, sound and visualization. In the beginning stages of practice, these components may be somewhat difficult to perform with consistency and coordination but with continued effort, they become a pleasurable experience which will bring you closer to your awareness of your Self. It is difficult to control the mind in the beginning. Many aspirants loose heart because they have not obtained the results they had anticipated. They either quit prematurely or jump to different techniques without giving sufficient time for the exercises to work. They do not understand that although on occasion, profound changes will occur in a short time, for the most part it's a gradual process.

The philosophy of meditation may seem foreign to you at first but if you reflect upon it you will discover that it holds great truth as well as great potential to assist you in discovering abiding peace and harmony in your life. When you begin to practice and discover how wonderful it is to be in control of your mind instead of being prey to the positive or negative emotions and desires you will discover an incomparable feeling which goes beyond the ordinary concept of happiness. As with other human endeavors, in order to gain success you need to study the philosophy intensively with great concentration and then practice it in your day to day life. Treat it as an experiment. The world and your life will not go away. Just ask yourself: What would happen if I was to become less attached and more in control of my mind? Follow the teachings and discover the inner resources you need to discover true happiness and to overcome the obstacles of life.

The practice of meditation requires regular and sustained practice. Failure is assured if there is no effort. Likewise, success is assured if there is sustained, regular effort. This is the key to accomplishing any goal in life and, enlightenment, is a goal like any other, albeit the highest goal. With respect to attaining the goal of enlightenment, all other goals are like dust blowing in the wind. The following instruction will serve as guidelines for meditation and is not intended to be a substitute for a competent instructor. There are many techniques of meditation. Here we will focus on basic techniques of "moving" meditations for initially calming the mind of the beginning practitioner.

Tips for Formal Meditation Practice

Begin by meditating for 5 minutes each day, gradually building up the time. The key is consistency in time and place. Nature inspires us to establish a set routine to perform our activities; the sun rises in the east and sets in the west every day, the moon's cycle is every 28 days and the seasons change approximately at the same times of the year, every year. It is better to practice for 5 minutes each day than 20 minutes one day and 0 minutes the next. Do a formal sit down meditation whenever the feeling comes to you but try to do it at least once a day, preferably between 4-6 am or 6-8 pm. Do not eat for at least 2 hours before meditation. It is even more preferable to not eat 12 hours before. For example: eat nothing (except only water or tea) after 6 p.m. until after meditation at 6 a.m. the following morning. Do not meditate within 24 hours of having sexual intercourse. Meditate alone or in a meditation group in a quiet area, in a dimly lit room (candle light is adequate). Do light exercise (example: Chi Kung or Hatha Yoga) before meditating, then say Hekau (affirmations, prayers, mantras, etc.) for a few minutes to set up positive vibrations in the mind. Burning your favorite incense is a good way to set the mood. Keep a ritualistic procedure about the meditation time. Do things in a slow, deliberate manner, concentrating on every motion and every thought you perform.

When ready, try to focus the mind on one object, symbol or idea such as the heart or Hetep (Supreme Peace). If the mind strays, bring it back gently. Patience, self-love and self-forgiveness are the keys here. Gradually, the mind will not drift toward thoughts or objects of the world. It will move toward subtler levels of consciousness until it reaches the source of the thoughts and there commune with that source, Neter Neteru. This is the desired positive movement of the practice of meditation because it is from Neter Neteru that all inspiration, creativity and altruistic feelings of love come. Neter Neteru is the source of peace and love and is who you really are.

Rituals and Prayers Associated With Meditation Practice

In the beginning the mind may be difficult to control. What is needed here is perseverance and the application of the techniques described here. Another important aid to meditation is ritualism. You should observe a set of rituals whenever you intend to practice meditation. These will gradually help to settle the mind even before you actually sit to practice the meditation. They are especially useful if you are a busy person or if you have many thoughts or worries on the mind. First take a bath. Water is the greatest cleanser of impurities. In ancient times the practitioners of yoga would bathe before entering the temples and engaging in the mystery rituals. This practice has been kept alive in the Christian practice of baptism and the prayers using the Holy Water. In the *Gospel of Peace,* water is used as an external as well as internal cleanser of the body. In modern times many Native American spiritual leaders and others use water as a means to transport negative vibrations in the body in the form of a restless mind, or other negative thoughts directed toward others or oneself out and away from the body. This may be accomplished by simply visualizing the negative feelings moving into the water as you bathe and then going down the drain and into the earth as the water is washed away. This is a very powerful means of purification because the mind controls the energies in the body. Therefore, if the mind is controlled, you will be able to control the energies of your body, your emotions, attitudes, etc. Use the images on page 64 if you do not have an altar.

Healing the Criminal Heart

Next invoke the assistance of the deity or cosmic force which removes obstacles to your success in spiritual practice. Anubis is the deity which leads souls through the narrow pathways of the Tuat. Therefore, request the assistance of Anubis, who represents the discriminative intellectual ability so that you may *"distinguish the real from the unreal."*

> *"O Apuat* (Anubis), *opener of the ways, the roads of the North, O Anpu, opener of the ways, the roads of the South. The messenger between heaven and hell displaying alternately a face black as night, and golden as the day. He is equally watchful by day as by night."*

> *"May Anubis make my thighs firm so that I may stand upon them."*

> *"I have washed myself in the water wherein the god Anpu washed when he performed the office of embalmer and bandager. My lips are the lips of Anpu."*

Next invoke the presence of Isis-Maat who is the embodiment of wisdom and inner discovery of the Divine. Isis (Aset) is the mother of the universe and she herself veils her true form, as the Supreme Transcendental Self. This "veil" of ignorance is only due to ignorance. Therefore, pray for Isis to make her presence, which bestows instant revelation of her true form. This "unveiling" is a metaphor symbolizing the intuitional revelation of the Divine or Enlightenment in your mind. Isis is in your heart and only needs to be revealed. However, she can only reveal herself to the true aspirant, one who is devoted to her (the Self) and her alone. Isis says: *"I Isis, am all that has been, all that is, or shall be; and no mortal man hath ever unveiled me."* The invocatory prayer to Isis is:

> *"Oh benevolent Aset, who protected her brother Asar, who searched for him without wearying, who traversed the land in mourning and never rested until she had found him. She who afforded him shadow with her wings and gave him air with her feathers, who rejoiced and carried her brother home.*
> *She who revived what was faint for the weary one, who received his seed and conceived an heir, and who nourished him in solitude while no one knew where he was. . . . "*

"I am the hawk (Heru) in the tabernacle, and I pierce through the veil."

Healing the Criminal Heart

Then remember your Spiritual Preceptor, the person who taught you how to meditate, thank them for their teaching and invoke their grace for success in your meditation. *"Have faith in your master's ability to lead you along the path of truth."*

> *"The lips of the wise are as the doors of a cabinet; no sooner are they opened, but treasures are poured out before you. Like unto trees of gold arranged in beds of silver, are wise sentences uttered in due season."*

Next, utter some invocatory prayers such as the Hymns of Amun to propitiate the benevolent presence of the Supreme Being. Visualize that with each utterance you are being enfolded in Divine Grace and Enlightenment.

> *O Åmen, O Åmen, who art in heaven, turn thy face upon the dead body of the child, and make your child sound and strong in the Underworld.*

> *O Åmen, O Åmen, O God, O God, O Åmen, I adore thy name, grant thou to me that I may understand thee; Grant thou that I may have peace in the Tuat, and that I may possess all my members therein...*

> *Hail, Åmen, let me make supplication unto thee, for I know thy name, and thy transformations are in my mouth, and thy skin is before my eyes. Come, I pray thee, and place thou thine heir and thine image, myself, in the everlasting underworld... let my whole body become like that of a neter, let me escape from the evil chamber and let me not be imprisoned therein; for I worship thy name...*

> *I am pure. I am pure. I am Pure.*
> *I have washed my front parts with the waters of libations, I have cleansed my hinder parts with drugs which make wholly clean, and my inward parts have been washed in the liquor of Maat.*

Now resolve within yourself that you will stay for the prescribed period of time which you have determined and then proceed with the practice as described below. Remember the following precepts: *"Have devotion of purpose"*, *"Have faith in your own ability to accept the truth"*, *"Have faith in your ability to act with wisdom."*

Devotional Prayer:

> *amma su en pa neter*
> *sauu - k su emment en pa neter*
> *au tuanu ma qeti pa haru*

> "Give thyself to GOD,
> keep thou thyself daily for God;

and let tomorrow be as today."

Devotional Prayer to Heru:

A HYMN TO HERU
(From the hieroglyphic text The Death of Horus)

"Heru is the savior who was brought to birth, as light in heaven and sustenance on earth. Horus in spirit, verily divine, who came to turn the water into wine. Horus who gave his life, and sowed the seed for men to make the bread of life indeed. Horus, the comforter, who did descend in human fashion as the heavenly friend. Horus, the word, the founder in youth, Horus, the fulfiller of the word made truth. Horus, the Lord and leader in the fight against the dark powers of the night. Horus, the sufferer with cross bowed down, who rose at Easter with his double crown. Horus the pioneer, who paved the way of resurrection to the eternal day. Horus triumphant with the battle done, Lord of two worlds, united and made one."

Horus says:

"I am the hawk in the tabernacle, and I pierce through the veil."

Devotional Prayer to Heru-Min:

A Hymn to Min from the Stele of Sobk-iry:

I worship Min, I extol arm-raising Horus:
Hail to you, Min in his processional
Tall-plumed, son of Osiris,
Born of divine Isis.
Great in Senut, mighty in Ipu,
You of Coptos, Horus strong-armed,
Lord of awe who silences pride,
Sovereign of all the gods
Fragrance laden when he comes from Medja-land,
Awe inspiring in Nubia,
You of Utent, hail and praise.

Devotional Prayer to Asar (Osiris:

A HYMN TO ASAR
(From the Book of Coming Forth By Day)

Healing the Criminal Heart

A HYMN OF PRAYER TO ASAR. "Glory to Osiris Un-Nefer, the great god within Abydos, king of eternity, lord of the everlasting, who passeth through millions of years in his existence. Eldest son of the womb of Nut, engendered by Geb, the chief lord of the crowns of the North and South, lord of the lofty white crown. As Prince of gods and of men he has received the crook and the flail and the dignity of his divine fathers[1]. Let thy heart which is in the mountain of Amenta be content, for thy son Horus is established upon thy throne. You are crowned lord of Djaddu[2] and ruler in Abtus[3]. Through thee the world waxeth green in triumph before the might of Neb-er-tcher[4]. He leadeth in his train that which is and that which is not yet, in his name Ta-her-seta-nef[5]; he toweth along the earth in triumph in his name Seker[6].

He is exceedingly mighty and most terrible in his name Osiris. He endureth forever and forever in his name Un-nefer[7]. Homage to thee, King of Kings, Lord of Lords, Prince of Princes, who from the womb of Nut have possessed the world and have ruled all lands and Akert[8]. Thy body is of gold, thy head is of azure, and emerald light encircleth thee. O An[9] of millions of years, all-pervading with thy body and beautiful in countenance in Ta-sert[10]. Grant thou to the Ka of Osiris, the initiate, splendor in heaven and might upon earth and triumph in Neter-khert; and that I may, sail down to Djaddu like a living soul and up to Abdu like a bennu (phoenix); and that I may go in and come out without repulse at the pylons of the Duat[10]. May there be given unto me loaves of bread in the house of coolness, and offerings of food in Annu[11] , and a homestead forever in Sekbet-Aru[12], with wheat and barley therefore..."

It has come to a good ending in Thebes, the place of truth.

Notes on the Hymn to Osiris (Asar)

1- Osiris, as the night sun (the moon) was also the sun of Ra.

2- Djaddu was the name of two towns in Ancient Egypt. In mystical terms it refers to being firmly established in the Netherworld. The Ancient Egyptian word Djaddu refers to "steadfastness" or "stability" as well as the pillar of Osiris. This is also being referred to in the following line from the *Egyptian Book of Coming Forth By Day*, Chapter I: 13-15:

nuk Djeddi, se Djeddi au am-a em Djeddu Mesi - a em Djeddu

"I am *Djeddi* (steadfast), son of *Djeddi* (steadfast), conceived and born in the region of *Djeddu* (steadfastness)."

3- *Abdu* was the city which the Greeks called *Abydos*. It is also reputed to be the resting place of the body of Osiris.

4- Nebertcher literally means "All Encompassing Divinity" or "Supreme Being".

5- The One who draws the world, i.e. Ra, the Supreme Being, who causes the world to exist by drawing it along in the movement of the Barque of "Millions of Years".

6- Seker is the divine form of the Supreme Being (Osiris, Ptah, Tenen) as the night sun, symbolizing the period of death.

7- The "Beautiful Being" or the "Good Being", i.e. Osiris.

8- The country of which Osiris is the ruler. There was an Akert or burial ground on the western side of the Nile. This is where many important excavations have been conducted in recent times, uncovering the tombs of Kings, Queens and Nobles of Ancient Egypt.

9- A name of the sun god, i.e. Ra (Osiris).

10- A name of the underworld.

11- The city of the sun, the first city which emerged with the creation, thus, the abode of Ra and the Ennead.

12- A section of the astral world. It is part of the *Sekhet-hetepu*, where souls of the blessed reap and sow.

Importance of Proper Breathing

Most people in the modern world do not know how to breathe properly. Most people (especially males) have learned to breathe by pushing out the chest in a "manly" or "macho" fashion. This mode of breathing is harmful for many reasons. The amount of air taken in is less and vital cosmic energy is reduced and becomes stagnant in the subtle vital energy channels, resulting in physical and mental diseases. The stagnation of the flow of energy through the body has the effect of grounding one's consciousness to the physical realities rather than allowing the mind and body to operate with lightness and subtlety.

"Belly breathing" or abdominal breathing massages the internal organs and develops Life Force energy (Ra, Chi or Kundalini). It will be noticed that it is our natural breathing pattern when we lie down on our back. Instruction is as follows: A- Breathe in and push the stomach out. B- Breathe out and pull the stomach in. This form of breathing is to be practiced at all times, not just during meditation. It allows the natural Life Force in the air to be rhythmically supplied to the body and nervous system. This process is indispensable in the achievement of physical health and mental-spiritual power to control the mind (meditation).

Practice proper breathing before your daily, monthly and annual worship exercises. Also, use the proper breathing technique whenever you feel stress or anxiety. You will find that it will calm you physically and mentally and you will be able to deal with the stress. Also, the daily worship and meditation program will work to reduce stress and bring mental clarity. Practice proper breathing as follows.

As you breath in allow your belly to move out and as you breath in bring the belly in towards your spine. As you breath in count 1, 2, 3, and 4. Hold for two counts 1 and 2. Then breath out for eight counts. 1, 2, 3, 4, 5, 6, 7, and 8. Repeat ten times.

You may also use this count as you practice meditation.

SIMPLE MEDITATION TECHNIQUE

Modern scientific research has proven that one of the most effective things anyone can do to promote mental and physical health is to sit quietly for 20 minutes twice each day. This is more effective than a change in diet, vitamins, food supplements, medicines, etc. It is not necessary to possess any special skill or training. All that is required is that one achieves a relaxed state of mind, unburdened by the duties of the day. You may sit from a few minutes up to an hour in the morning and in the late afternoon.

This simple practice, if followed each day, will promote above average physical health and spiritual evolution. One's mental and emotional health will be maintained in a healthy state as well. The most important thing to remember during this meditation time is to just relax and not try to stop the mind from pursuing a particular idea but also not trying to actively make the mind pursue a particular thought or idea. If a Hekau or Mantra (Prayer) is recited, or if a special hieroglyph is meditated upon, the mind should not be forced to hold it. Rather, one should direct the mind and when one realizes that one has been carried away with a particular thought, bring the mind gently back to the original object of meditation, in this way, it will eventually settle where it feels most comfortable and at peace.

Sometimes one will know that one has been carried away into thoughts about what one needs to do, or who needs to be called, or is something burning in the kitchen?, etc. These thoughts are worldly thoughts. Simply bring the mind back to the original object of meditation or the hekau. With more practice, the awareness of the hekau or object of meditation (candle, mandala, etc.) will dissipate as you go deeper. This is the positive, meditative movement that is desired. The goal is to relax to such a degree that the mind drifts to deeper and deeper levels of consciousness, finally reaching the source of consciousness, the source of all thought; then the mind transcends even this level of consciousness and there, communes with the Absolute Reality, Neter. This is the state of "Cosmic Consciousness", the state of enlightenment. After a while, the mental process will remain at the Soul level all the time. This is the Enlightened Sage Level.

WORDS OF POWER IN MEDITATION: Khu-Hekau, Mantra Repetition:

Chanting Words of Power is a potent way to purify the mind. The word *"mantra"* in Indian Yoga signifies any sound which steadies the mind. Its roots are: "man" which means "mind" and "tra" which means "steady." In Ancient Egyptian terminology, "hekau" or word formulas are recited with meaning and feeling to achieve the desired end.

Hekau-mantra recitation, (called *Japa* in India), is especially useful in changing the mental state. The sounds coupled with ideas or meditations based on a profound understanding of the meaning can have the effect of calming the mind by directing its energy toward sublime thoughts rather than toward degrading, pain filled ones. This allows the vibrations of the mind to be changed. There are three types of recitations that can be used with the words of power: 1- Mental, 2- Recitation employing a soft humming sound and 3- loud or audible reciting. The main purpose of reciting the words of power is somewhat different than prayer. Prayer involves you as a subject, "talking" to God, while words of power - hekau - mantras, are used to carry your consciousness to divine levels by changing the vibrations in your mind and allowing it to transcend the awareness of the senses, body and ordinary thought processes.

The recitation of words of power has been explored to such a degree that it constitutes an important form of yoga practice. Two of the most comprehensive books written on this subject by Sri Swami Sivananda were *Japa Yoga* and *Sadhana*. Swami Sivananda told his pupils to repeat their mantras as many as 50,000 per day. If this level of practice is maintained, it is possible to achieve specific changes in a short time. Otherwise, changes in your level of mental awareness, self-control, mental peace and spiritual realization occur according to your level of practice. You should not rush nor suppress your spiritual development, rather allow it to gradually grow into a fire which engulfs the mind as your spiritual aspiration grows in a natural way.

Hekau-mantras can be directed toward worldly attainments or toward spiritual attainment in the form of enlightenment. There are words of power for gaining wealth or control over others. We will present Egyptian, Indian and Christian words of power which are directed to self-control and mental peace leading to spiritual realization of the Higher Self. You may choose from the list according to your level of understanding and practice. If you were initiated into a particular hekau or mantra by an authentic spiritual preceptor, we recommend that you use that one as your main meditative sound formula. You may use others for singing according to your inclination in your leisure or idle time. Also you may use shortened versions for chanting or singing when not engaged in formal practice. For example, if you choose "Om Amun Ra Ptah", you may also use "Om Amun."

Reciting words of power is like making a well. If a well is made deep enough, it yields water. If the words of power are used long enough and with consistency, they yield spiritual vibrations which reach deep into the unconscious mind to cut through the distracting thoughts and then reveal the deeper you. If they are not used with consistency, they are like shallow puddles which get filled easily by rain, not having had a chance to go deeply enough to reveal what lies within. Don't forget that your movement in yoga should be balanced and integrated. Therefore, continue your practice of the other major disciplines we have described along with your practice of reciting the hekau-mantras. Mental recitation is considered to be the most powerful. However, in the beginning you may need to start with recitation aloud until you are able to control the mind's wandering. If it wanders, simply return to the words of power (hekau-mantras). Eventually the words of power will develop their own staying power. You will even hear them when you are not consciously reciting. They will begin to replace the negative thought patterns of the mind and lead the mind toward serenity and from here to spiritual realization. When this occurs you should allow yourself to feel the sweetness of reciting the divine names.

As discussed earlier, HEKAU may be used to achieve control over the mind and to develop the latent forces that are within you. Hekau or mantras are mystic formulas which an aspirant uses in a process of self-alchemy. The chosen words of power may be in the form of a letter, word or a combination of words which hold a specific mystical meaning to lead the mind to deeper levels of concentration and to deeper levels of understanding of the teaching behind the words. You may choose one for yourself or you my use one that you were initiated into by a spiritual preceptor. Also, you may have a special hekau for meditation and you may still use other hekau, prayers, hymns or songs of praise according to your devotional feeling. Once you choose a hekau, the practice involves its repetition with meaning and feeling to the point of becoming one with it. You will experience that the words of power drop from your mind and there are no thoughts but just awareness. This is the soul level where you begin to transcend thoughts and body identification. You may begin practicing it out loud (verbally) and later practice in silence (mentally). At some point your level of concentration will deepen. You may use a rosary or "mala" (beads on a string) to keep track of your recitation. At that point your mind will disengage from all external exercises and take flight into the unknown, uncharted waters of the subconscious, the unconscious, and beyond. Simply remain as a detached witness and allow yourself to grow in peace. Listed below are several hekau taken from ancient Egyptian texts. They may be used in English or in ancient Kemetic according to your choice.

If you feel a certain affinity toward a particular energy expressed through a particular deity, use that inclination to your advantage by aligning yourself with that energy and then directing it toward the divine within your heart. Never forget that while you are working with a particular deity in the beginning stages, your objective is to delve into the deeper mystical implications of the symbolic form and characteristics of the deity. These always refer to the transcendental Self which is beyond all deities. According to your level of advancement you may construct your own Hekau according to your own feeling and understanding. As a rule, in meditations such as those being discussed now, the shorter the size of the hekau the more effective it will be since you will be able repeat it more often. However, the shorter the hekau, the more concentration it requires so as not to get lost in thoughts. You may wish to begin with a longer hekau and shorten it as your concentration builds. Words of power have no power in and of themselves. It is the user who gives them power through understanding and feeling.

Om is a powerful word. It is present in the Ancient Egyptian Amon, the Christian Amun and the Jewish Shalom and in other cultures through the special use of the *"m."* While *Om* is most commonly known as a *Sanskrit* mantra (word of power from India), it also appears in the ancient Egyptian texts and is closely related to the Kemetic *Amun* in sound and Amun of Christianity. More importantly, it has the same meaning as Amun and is therefore completely compatible with the energy pattern of the entire group. According to the Egyptian Leyden papyrus, the name of the "Hidden God", referring to Amun, may be pronounced as *Om,* or *Am*.

Om is a powerful sound; it represents the primordial sound of creation. Thus it appears in ancient Egypt as Om, in modern day India as Om, and in Christianity as Amun, being derived from Amun. Om may also be used for engendering mental calm prior to beginning recitation of a longer set of words of power or it may be used alone as described above. One Indian Tantric scripture (*Tattva Prakash*) states that Om or AUM can be used to achieve the mental state free of physical identification and can bring union with *Brahman* (the Absolute transcendental Supreme Being - God) if it is repeated 300,000 times. In this sense, mantras such as Om, Soham, Sivoham, Aham Brahmasmi are called *Moksha Mantras* or mantras which lead to union with the Absolute Self. Their shortness promotes greater concentration and force toward the primordial level of consciousness.

Simply choose a hekau which you feel comfortable with and sit quietly to recite it continuously for a set amount of time. Allow it to gradually become part of your free time when you are not concentrating on anything specific or when you are being distracted by worldly thoughts. This will serve to counteract the worldly or subconscious vibrations that may emerge from the your own unconscious mind. When you feel anger or other negative qualities, recite the hekau and visualize its energy and the deity associated with it destroying the negativity within you.

You may use the following Hekau for your spiritual practice.

"Om"
(The All, God, The Self, The Supreme Being)

"Om Maati am Maak-heru"
(The Divine Self manifesting as Maati, grant that I become purified and enlightened)

"Ra-Maa
(The Divine Self Manifesting as Ra and Maat)

amma su en pa neter sauu - k su emment en pa neter
au tuanu ma qeti pa haru

"Give thyself to GOD, keep thou thyself daily for God;
and let tomorrow be as today."

You may use any of the proverbs contained throughout this book for meditation or reflection-study of the teachings.

HOLIDAYS AND SPECIAL OBSERVANCES OF SHETAUT NETER

The following are some of the important holidays of the Shetaut Neter Religion. Also included are observances and practices to be performed on those special days.

DAILY WORSHIP:

Morning prayers and meditation
Noon prayer and meditation
Evening prayer and meditation

MONTHLY WORSHIP:

1st day of the month is Festival day.
15th day of the month is Festival day.

Fourteen days of Waning Moon: Day 1 to 14. Dismemberment and death of Asar. Daily readings from the first half of the Ausarian Resurrection Myth. —see the book Resurrecting Osiris

Fourteen days of Waxing Moon: Day 15 to 31. Reconstitution and resurrection of Asar. Daily readings from the second half of the Ausarian Resurrection Myth. —see the book Resurrecting Osiris

Full Moon Days: Worship of Heru. Daily readings from the Hymns to Heru.

ANNUAL WORSHIP:

SECOND HALF OF JULY: RISING OF SIRIUS: Worship of the Goddess

Daily readings of the Story of Ra and Aset and the Story of Het-hor and Djehuti—see the book Mysticism of Ushet Rekhat.

RESURRECTION OF ASAR AND BIRTH OF HERU: December 25th.

MYSTICISM OF USHET REKHAT: WORSHIP OF THE GODDESS: DEC. 22-26
Daily readings from the Litany of Aset and Nebethet —see the book *The Goddess Path*.

"Ra neb Aru"

THE BASIC DAILY DISCIPLINES OF SHETAUT NETER

- <u>Daily Shedy -Threefold daily worship</u> – Basic Discipline for the morning at Dawn

  - o Worship Ritual - Complete
    - Divine Song
    - Sema Yoga Postures
    - Reciting of the Great Realizations
    - Reading of scripture from one of the assigned Neterian Traditions
    - Chant – words of scripture
    - Meditation
    - Offering

  - o Worship Ritual – Noon and Dusk
    - Reciting of the Great Realizations
    - Divine Chant
    - Meditation

For worship the aspirant needs:
1. *Scroll with four truths and meditation chant*
2. *ankh*
3. *candle*
4. *prayer mat*

The Monthly Observances Shetaut Neter

- <u>Monthly Observances -</u> Twice monthly moon festival

    o New Moon Fasting 1 day
    o Full Moon Fasting 1 day

"Renput Aru"

The Annual Observances Shetaut Neter

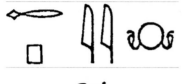

Api
Summer Solstice

Nun
Winterer Solstice

- <u>B</u>

<u>iannual Festival-ritual days</u>
- o Solstaces - Annual solar festivals
  - Fasting 3 days
  - Worship Ritual - Complete for Dawn, Noon and Dusk disciplines.

"Ahau"

The Lifetime Observances Shetaut Neter

- Pilgrimage to Egypt
  - o To be guided by Hm / Hmt or higher order priest or priestess

The General Principles of Shetaut Neter

1. The Purpose of Life is to Attain the Great Awakening-Enlightenment-Know thyself.
2. SHETAUT NETER enjoins the Shedy (spiritual investigation) as the highest endeavor of life.
3. SHETAUT NETER enjoins the responsibility of every human being is to promote order and truth.
4. SHETAUT NETER enjoins the performance of Selfless Service to family, community and humanity.
5. SHETAUT NETER enjoins the Protection of nature.
6. SHETAUT NETER enjoins the Protection of the weak and oppressed.
7. SHETAUT NETER enjoins the Caring for hungry.
8. SHETAUT NETER enjoins the Caring for homeless.
9. SHETAUT NETER enjoins the equality for all people.
10. SHETAUT NETER enjoins the equality between men and women.
11. SHETAUT NETER enjoins the justice for all.
12. SHETAUT NETER enjoins the sharing of resources.
13. SHETAUT NETER enjoins the protection and proper raising of children.
14. SHETAUT NETER enjoins the movement towards balance and peace.

May the grace of the Divine Mother be upon you.

Anyone who is seriously and sincerely interested in studying the path of Maat should begin by reading and applying the teachings presented in the book: *The Wisdom of Maati* by Dr. Muata Ashby. The Egyptian Yoga Book Series has been created for those who would like to explore the various paths of Yoga science from the Ancient Egyptian perspective. However, Maat is the foundation of all other paths because the practice of Maat purifies the heart and allows a person to become a vessel for higher spiritual realization. Therefore, a person who has experienced adversity in life must realize that they are the cause of their own misery but that through proper feeling, thinking and action they can rise above error, doubt and sinfulness (negativity).

For further study and spiritual practice see the books
THE WISDOM OF MAATI:
Spiritual Enlightenment Through the Path of Virtue
196 pages 5.5"x 8.5" ISBN 1-884564-20-8 $15.99

THE AUSARIAN RESURRECTION:
The Ancient Egyptian Bible
210 Pages 8.5" X 11" Soft Cover ISBN: 1-884564-27-5 $18.99 U.S.

INITIATION INTO EGYPTIAN YOGA:
The Secrets of Shedi
150 pages 8.5" X 11" ISBN 1-884564-02-X   Soft Cover $16.99 U.S.

Index

Kingdom, 12, 16, 20, 33, 133
Kingdom of Heaven, 12, 20, 133
KMT (Ancient Egypt). See also
  Kamit, 13, 29
Krishna, 133
Kundalini, 4, 9, 10
Kush, 28, 29, 33
Liberation, 12, 20
Libyans, 16
Life Force, 99, 130
Love, 3, 8, 129
Maat, 8, 23, 35, 73, 74, 99, 100,
  129, 132, 133
MAAT, 129
MAATI, 129
Manetho, 16, 17, 25
Manetho, see also History of
  Manetho, 25
Manu, 99
Matter, 132
Meditation, 127, 129, 130, 140
Memphis, 19
Men-nefer, see also Het-Ka-Ptah,
  Memphis, 19
Mesopotamia, 21
Metaphysics, 132
Middle East, 32, 126
Middle Kingdom, 16
Min, 130
Mind, 10
Moon, 13
Moses, 17
Music, 4, 9, 99, 139, 140
Mysteries, 128, 134
Mysticism, 8, 9, 12, 28, 128, 131,
  132, 134
Mythology, 12, 28
Neberdjer, 97, 99
Nefer, 138, 140

Neolithic, 23
Nephthys, 35
Net, goddess, 19
Neter, 10, 12, 28, 131
Neteru, 138, 139, 140
New Kingdom, 16, 33
Nile River, 16
North East Africa . See also Egypt
  Ethiopia
    Cush, 15, 18
North East Africa. See also
  Egypt
  Ethiopia
    Cush, 18
Nubia, 28, 29, 34
Nubian, 16, 28, 34
Nubians, 14, 30, 32, 34
Nut, 35, 99, 131
Octavian, 16
Old Kingdom, 16
Om, 139, 140
Orion Star Constellation, 132
Orthodox, 23, 25
Osiris, 19, 35, 131, 139, 140
Palermo Stone, 16, 25
Papyrus of Turin, 16, 25
Peace (see also Hetep), 10
Persia, 14, 30
PERT EM HERU, SEE ALSO BOOK
  OF THE DEAD, 131
Petrie, Flinders, 33
Pharaonic headdress, 24
Philae, 19, 131
Philosophy, 3, 4, 8, 9, 12, 15, 26, 28,
  30, 35, 100, 128, 129, 131,
  132, 133
Priests and Priestesses, 128
Proverbs, 4
Ptah, 19, 35, 132

Other Books From C M Books

P.O.Box 570459
Miami, Florida, 33257
(305) 378-6253 Fax: (305) 378-6253

This book is part of a series on the study and practice of Ancient Egyptian Yoga and Mystical Spirituality based on the writings of Dr. Muata Abhaya Ashby. They are also part of the Egyptian Yoga Course provided by the Sema Institute of Yoga. Below you will find a listing of the other books in this series. For more information send for the Egyptian Yoga Book-Audio-Video Catalog or the Egyptian Yoga Course Catalog.

Now you can study the teachings of Egyptian and Indian Yoga wisdom and Spirituality with the Egyptian Yoga Mystical Spirituality Series. The Egyptian Yoga Series takes you through the Initiation process and lead you to understand the mysteries of the soul and the Divine and to attain the highest goal of life: ENLIGHTENMENT. The *Egyptian Yoga Series*, takes you on an in depth study of Ancient Egyptian mythology and their inner mystical meaning. Each Book is prepared for the serious student of the mystical sciences and provides a study of the teachings along with exercises, assignments and projects to make the teachings understood and effective in real life. The Series is part of the Egyptian Yoga course but may be purchased even if you are not taking the course. The series is ideal for study groups.

Prices subject to change.

1. EGYPTIAN YOGA: THE PHILOSOPHY OF ENLIGHTENMENT An original, fully illustrated work, including hieroglyphs, detailing the meaning of the Egyptian mysteries, tantric yoga, psycho-spiritual and physical exercises. Egyptian Yoga is a guide to the practice of the highest spiritual philosophy which leads to absolute freedom from human misery and to immortality. It is well known by scholars that Egyptian philosophy is the basis of Western and Middle Eastern religious philosophies such as *Christianity, Islam, Judaism,* the *Kabala*, and Greek philosophy, but what about Indian philosophy, Yoga and Taoism? What were the original teachings? How can they be practiced today? What is the source of pain and suffering in the world and what is the solution? Discover the deepest mysteries of the mind and universe within and outside of your self. 8.5" X 11" ISBN: 1-884564-01-1 Soft $19.95

2. EGYPTIAN YOGA II: The Supreme Wisdom of Enlightenment by Dr. Muata Ashby ISBN 1-884564-39-9 $23.95 U.S. In this long awaited sequel to *Egyptian Yoga: The Philosophy of Enlightenment* you will take a fascinating and

enlightening journey back in time and discover the teachings which constituted the epitome of Ancient Egyptian spiritual wisdom. What are the disciplines which lead to the fulfillment of all desires? Delve into the three states of consciousness (waking, dream and deep sleep) and the fourth state which transcends them all, Neberdjer, "The Absolute." These teachings of the city of Waset (Thebes) were the crowning achievement of the Sages of Ancient Egypt. They establish the standard mystical keys for understanding the profound mystical symbolism of the Triad of human consciousness.

3. THE KEMETIC DIET: GUIDE TO HEALTH, DIET AND FASTING Health issues have always been important to human beings since the beginning of time. The earliest records of history show that the art of healing was held in high esteem since the time of Ancient Egypt. In the early 20th century, medical doctors had almost attained the status of sainthood by the promotion of the idea that they alone were "scientists" while other healing modalities and traditional healers who did not follow the "scientific method' were nothing but superstitious, ignorant charlatans who at best would take the money of their clients and at worst kill them with the unscientific "snake oils" and "irrational theories". In the late 20th century, the failure of the modern medical establishment's ability to lead the general public to good health, promoted the move by many in society towards "alternative medicine". Alternative medicine disciplines are those healing modalities which do not adhere to the philosophy of allopathic medicine. Allopathic medicine is what medical doctors practice by an large. It is the theory that disease is caused by agencies outside the body such as bacteria, viruses or physical means which affect the body. These can therefore be treated by medicines and therapies The natural healing method began in the absence of extensive technologies with the idea that all the answers for health may be found in nature or rather, the deviation from nature. Therefore, the health of the body can be restored by correcting the aberration and thereby restoring balance. This is the area that will be covered in this volume. Allopathic techniques have their place in the art of healing. However, we should not forget that the body is a grand achievement of the spirit and built into it is the capacity to maintain itself and heal itself. Ashby, Muata ISBN: 1-884564-49-6 $28.95

4. INITIATION INTO EGYPTIAN YOGA Shedy: Spiritual discipline or program, to go deeply into the mysteries, to study the mystery teachings and literature profoundly, to penetrate the mysteries. You will learn about the mysteries of initiation into the teachings and practice of Yoga and how to become an Initiate of the mystical sciences. This insightful manual is the first in a series which introduces you to the goals of daily spiritual and yoga practices: Meditation, Diet, Words of Power and the ancient wisdom teachings. 8.5" X 11" ISBN 1-884564-02-X Soft Cover $24.95 U.S.

5. *THE AFRICAN ORIGINS OF CIVILIZATION, MYSTICAL RELIGION AND YOGA PHILOSOPHY* HARD COVER EDITION ISBN: 1-884564-50-X

Healing the Criminal Heart

$80.00 U.S.   81/2" X 11"   Part 1, Part 2, Part 3 in one volume 683 Pages Hard Cover First Edition Three volumes in one. Over the past several years I have been asked to put together in one volume the most important evidences showing the correlations and common teachings between Kamitan (Ancient Egyptian) culture and religion and that of India. The questions of the history of Ancient Egypt, and the latest archeological evidences showing civilization and culture in Ancient Egypt and its spread to other countries, has intrigued many scholars as well as mystics over the years. Also, the possibility that Ancient Egyptian Priests and Priestesses migrated to Greece, India and other countries to carry on the traditions of the Ancient Egyptian Mysteries, has been speculated over the years as well. In chapter 1 of the book *Egyptian Yoga The Philosophy of Enlightenment,* 1995, I first introduced the deepest comparison between Ancient Egypt and India that had been brought forth up to that time. Now, in the year 2001 this new book, *THE AFRICAN ORIGINS OF CIVILIZATION, MYSTICAL RELIGION AND YOGA PHILOSOPHY,* more fully explores the motifs, symbols and philosophical correlations between Ancient Egyptian and Indian mysticism and clearly shows not only that Ancient Egypt and India were connected culturally but also spiritually. How does this knowledge help the spiritual aspirant? This discovery has great importance for the Yogis and mystics who follow the philosophy of Ancient Egypt and the mysticism of India. It means that India has a longer history and heritage than was previously understood. It shows that the mysteries of Ancient Egypt were essentially a yoga tradition which did not die but rather developed into the modern day systems of Yoga technology of India. It further shows that African culture developed Yoga Mysticism earlier than any other civilization in history. All of this expands our understanding of the unity of culture and the deep legacy of Yoga, which stretches into the distant past, beyond the Indus Valley civilization, the earliest known high culture in India as well as the Vedic tradition of Aryan culture. Therefore, Yoga culture and mysticism is the oldest known tradition of spiritual development and Indian mysticism is an extension of the Ancient Egyptian mysticism. By understanding the legacy which Ancient Egypt gave to India the mysticism of India is better understood and by comprehending the heritage of Indian Yoga, which is rooted in Ancient Egypt the Mysticism of Ancient Egypt is also better understood. This expanded understanding allows us to prove the underlying kinship of humanity, through the common symbols, motifs and philosophies which are not disparate and confusing teachings but in reality expressions of the same study of truth through metaphysics and mystical realization of Self. (HARD COVER)

6.   AFRICAN ORIGINS BOOK 1 PART 1 African Origins of African Civilization, Religion, Yoga Mysticism and Ethics Philosophy-Soft Cover $24.95 ISBN: 1-884564-55-0

7.   AFRICAN ORIGINS BOOK 2 PART 2 African Origins of Western Civilization, Religion and Philosophy(Soft) -Soft Cover $24.95 ISBN: 1-884564-56-9

8.   EGYPT AND INDIA (AFRICAN ORIGINS BOOK 3 PART 3) African Origins of
        Eastern Civilization, Religion, Yoga Mysticism and Philosophy-<u>Soft Cover</u>
        $29.95 (Soft) ISBN: 1-884564-57-7

9.   THE MYSTERIES OF ISIS: **The Ancient Egyptian Philosophy of Self-
        Realization** - There are several paths to discover the Divine and the mysteries of
        the higher Self. This volume details the mystery teachings of the goddess Aset
        (Isis) from Ancient Egypt- the path of wisdom. It includes the teachings of her
        temple and the disciplines that are enjoined for the initiates of the temple of Aset
        as they were given in ancient times. Also, this book includes the teachings of the
        main myths of Aset that lead a human being to spiritual enlightenment and
        immortality. Through the study of ancient myth and the illumination of initiatic
        understanding the idea of God is expanded from the mythological
        comprehension to the metaphysical. Then this metaphysical understanding is
        related to you, the student, so as to begin understanding your true divine nature.
        ISBN 1-884564-24-0 $22.99

10.   EGYPTIAN PROVERBS: TEMT TCHAAS *Temt Tchaas* means: collection of
        ———Ancient Egyptian Proverbs How to live according to MAAT Philosophy.
        Beginning Meditation. All proverbs are indexed for easy searches. For the first
        time in one volume, ———Ancient Egyptian Proverbs, wisdom teachings and
        meditations, fully illustrated with hieroglyphic text and symbols. EGYPTIAN
        PROVERBS is a unique collection of knowledge and wisdom which you can put
        into practice today and transform your life. 5.5"x 8.5" $14.95 U.S   ISBN:
        1-884564-00-3

11.   THE PATH OF DIVINE LOVE The Process of Mystical Transformation and
        The Path of Divine Love   This Volume focuses on the ancient wisdom
        teachings of "Neter Merri" –the Ancient Egyptian philosophy of Divine Love
        and how to use them in a scientific process for self-transformation. Love is one
        of the most powerful human emotions. It is also the source of Divine feeling that
        unifies God and the individual human being. When love is fragmented and
        diminished by egoism the Divine connection is lost. The Ancient tradition of
        Neter Merri leads human beings back to their Divine connection, allowing them
        to discover their innate glorious self that is actually Divine and immortal. This
        volume will detail the process of transformation from ordinary consciousness to
        cosmic consciousness through the integrated practice of the teachings and the
        path of Devotional Love toward the Divine. 5.5"x 8.5" ISBN 1-884564-11-9
        $22.99

12.   INTRODUCTION TO MAAT PHILOSOPHY: Spiritual Enlightenment
        Through the Path of Virtue   Known as Karma Yoga in India, the teachings of
        MAAT for living virtuously and with orderly wisdom are explained and the
        student is to begin practicing the precepts of Maat in daily life so as to promote
        the process of purification of the heart in preparation for the judgment of the

soul. This judgment will be understood not as an event that will occur at the time of death but as an event that occurs continuously, at every moment in the life of the individual. The student will learn how to become allied with the forces of the Higher Self and to thereby begin cleansing the mind (heart) of impurities so as to attain a higher vision of reality. ISBN 1-884564-20-8 $22.99

13.   MEDITATION The Ancient Egyptian Path to Enlightenment   Many people do not know about the rich history of meditation practice in Ancient Egypt. This volume outlines the theory of meditation and presents the Ancient Egyptian Hieroglyphic text which give instruction as to the nature of the mind and its three modes of expression. It also presents the texts which give instruction on the practice of meditation for spiritual Enlightenment and unity with the Divine. This volume allows the reader to begin practicing meditation by explaining, in easy to understand terms, the simplest form of meditation and working up to the most advanced form which was practiced in ancient times and which is still practiced by yogis around the world in modern times. ISBN 1-884564-27-7 $24.99

14.   THE GLORIOUS LIGHT MEDITATION TECHNIQUE OF ANCIENT EGYPT ISBN: 1-884564-15-1$14.95 (PB) New for the year 2000. This volume is based on the earliest known instruction in history given for the practice of formal meditation. Discovered by Dr. Muata Ashby, it is inscribed on the walls of the Tomb of Seti I in Thebes Egypt. This volume details the philosophy and practice of this unique system of meditation originated in Ancient Egypt and the earliest practice of meditation known in the world which occurred in the most advanced African Culture.

15.   THE SERPENT POWER: The Ancient Egyptian Mystical Wisdom of the Inner Life Force.   This Volume specifically deals with the latent life Force energy of the universe and in the human body, its control and sublimation. How to develop the Life Force energy of the subtle body. This Volume will introduce the esoteric wisdom of the science of how virtuous living acts in a subtle and mysterious way to cleanse the latent psychic energy conduits and vortices of the spiritual body. ISBN 1-884564-19-4 $22.95

16.   EGYPTIAN YOGA *The Postures of The Gods and Goddesses* Discover the physical postures and exercises practiced thousands of years ago in Ancient Egypt which are today known as Yoga exercises. This work is based on the pictures and teachings from the Creation story of Ra, The Asarian Resurrection Myth and the carvings and reliefs from various Temples in Ancient Egypt 8.5" X 11" ISBN 1-884564-10-0 Soft Cover $21.95   Exercise video $20

17.   EGYPTIAN TANTRA YOGA: The Art of Sex Sublimation and Universal Consciousness This Volume will expand on the male and female principles within the human body and in the universe and further detail the sublimation of sexual energy into spiritual energy. The student will study the deities Min and

Hathor, Asar and Aset, Geb and Nut and discover the mystical implications for a practical spiritual discipline. This Volume will also focus on the Tantric aspects of Ancient Egyptian and Indian mysticism, the purpose of sex and the mystical teachings of sexual sublimation which lead to self-knowledge and Enlightenment. 5.5"x 8.5" ISBN 1-884564-03-8 $24.95

18.   ASARIAN RELIGION: RESURRECTING OSIRIS The path of Mystical Awakening and the Keys to Immortality NEW REVISED AND EXPANDED EDITION! The Ancient Sages created stories based on human and superhuman beings whose struggles, aspirations, needs and desires ultimately lead them to discover their true Self. The myth of Aset, Asar and Heru is no exception in this area. While there is no one source where the entire story may be found, pieces of it are inscribed in various ancient Temples walls, tombs, steles and papyri. For the first time available, the complete myth of Asar, Aset and Heru has been compiled from original Ancient Egyptian, Greek and Coptic Texts. This epic myth has been richly illustrated with reliefs from the Temple of Heru at Edfu, the Temple of Aset at Philae, the Temple of Asar at Abydos, the Temple of Hathor at Denderah and various papyri, inscriptions and reliefs. Discover the myth which inspired the teachings of the *Shetaut Neter* (Egyptian Mystery System - Egyptian Yoga) and the Egyptian Book of Coming Forth By Day. Also, discover the three levels of Ancient Egyptian Religion, how to understand the mysteries of the Duat or Astral World and how to discover the abode of the Supreme in the Amenta, *The Other World*   The ancient religion of Asar, Aset and Heru, if properly understood, contains all of the elements necessary to lead the sincere aspirant to attain immortality through inner self-discovery. This volume presents the entire myth and explores the main mystical themes and rituals associated with the myth for understating human existence, creation and the way to achieve spiritual emancipation - *Resurrection.* The Asarian myth is so powerful that it influenced and is still having an effect on the major world religions. Discover the origins and mystical meaning of the Christian Trinity, the Eucharist ritual and the ancient origin of the birthday of Jesus Christ. Soft Cover ISBN: 1-884564-27-5 $24.95

19.   THE EGYPTIAN BOOK OF THE DEAD MYSTICISM OF THE PERT EM HERU $28.95   ISBN# 1-884564-28-3 Size: 8½" X 11" I Know myself, I know myself, I am One With God!–From the Pert Em Heru "The Ru Pert em Heru" or "Ancient Egyptian Book of The Dead," or "Book of Coming Forth By Day" as it is more popularly known, has fascinated the world since the successful translation of Ancient Egyptian hieroglyphic scripture over 150 years ago. The astonishing writings in it reveal that the Ancient Egyptians believed in life after death and in an ultimate destiny to discover the Divine. The elegance and aesthetic beauty of the hieroglyphic text itself has inspired many see it as an art form in and of itself. But is there more to it than that? Did the Ancient Egyptian wisdom contain more than just aphorisms and hopes of eternal life beyond death? In this volume Dr. Muata Ashby, the author of over 25 books on Ancient Egyptian Yoga Philosophy has produced a new translation of the

original texts which uncovers a mystical teaching underlying the sayings and rituals instituted by the Ancient Egyptian Sages and Saints. "Once the philosophy of Ancient Egypt is understood as a mystical tradition instead of as a religion or primitive mythology, it reveals its secrets which if practiced today will lead anyone to discover the glory of spiritual self-discovery. The Pert em Heru is in every way comparable to the Indian Upanishads or the Tibetan Book of the Dead." Muata Abhaya Ashby

20. ANUNIAN THEOLOGY THE MYSTERIES OF RA The Philosophy of Anu and The Mystical Teachings of The Ancient Egyptian Creation Myth Discover the mystical teachings contained in the Creation Myth and the gods and goddesses who brought creation and human beings into existence. The Creation Myth holds the key to understanding the universe and for attaining spiritual Enlightenment. ISBN: 1-884564-38-0 40 pages $14.95

21. MYSTERIES OF MIND Mystical Psychology & Mental Health for Enlightenment and Immortality based on the Ancient Egyptian Philosophy of Menefer -Mysticism of Ptah, Egyptian Physics and Yoga Metaphysics and the Hidden properties of Matter.   This volume uncovers the mystical psychology of the Ancient Egyptian wisdom teachings centering on the philosophy of the Ancient Egyptian city of Menefer (Memphite Theology). How to understand the mind and how to control the senses and lead the mind to health, clarity and mystical self-discovery. This Volume will also go deeper into the philosophy of God as creation and will explore the concepts of modern science and how they correlate with ancient teachings. This Volume will lay the ground work for the understanding of the philosophy of universal consciousness and the initiatic/yogic insight into who or what is God? ISBN 1-884564-07-0 $22.95

22. THE GODDESS AND THE EGYPTIAN MYSTERIESTHE PATH OF THE GODDESS THE GODDESS PATH The Secret Forms of the Goddess and the Rituals of Resurrection The Supreme Being may be worshipped as father or as mother. *Ushet Rekhat* or *Mother Worship*, is the spiritual process of worshipping the Divine in the form of the Divine Goddess. It celebrates the most important forms of the Goddess including *Nathor, Maat, Aset, Arat, Amentet and Hathor* and explores their mystical meaning as well as the rising of *Sirius,* the star of Aset (Aset) and the new birth of Hor (Heru). The end of the year is a time of reckoning, reflection and engendering a new or renewed positive movement toward attaining spiritual Enlightenment. The Mother Worship devotional meditation ritual, performed on five days during the month of December and on New Year's Eve, is based on the Ushet Rekhit. During the ceremony, the cosmic forces, symbolized by Sirius - and the constellation of Orion ---, are harnessed through the understanding and devotional attitude of the participant. This propitiation draws the light of wisdom and health to all those who share in the ritual, leading to prosperity and wisdom. $14.95 ISBN 1-884564-18-6

23.   *THE MYSTICAL JOURNEY FROM JESUS TO CHRIST* $24.95   ISBN# 1-884564-05-4 size: 8½" X 11" Discover the ancient Egyptian origins of Christianity before the Catholic Church and learn the mystical teachings given by Jesus to assist all humanity in becoming Christlike. Discover the secret meaning of the Gospels that were discovered in Egypt. Also discover how and why so many Christian churches came into being. Discover that the Bible still holds the keys to mystical realization even though its original writings were changed by the church. Discover how to practice the original teachings of Christianity which leads to the Kingdom of Heaven.

24.   THE STORY OF ASAR, ASET AND HERU: An Ancient Egyptian Legend (For Children)   Now for the first time, the most ancient myth of Ancient Egypt comes alive for children. Inspired by the books *The Asarian Resurrection: The Ancient Egyptian Bible* and *The Mystical Teachings of The Asarian Resurrection, The Story of Asar, Aset and Heru* is an easy to understand and thrilling tale which inspired the children of Ancient Egypt to aspire to greatness and righteousness.   If you and your child have enjoyed stories like *The Lion King* and *Star Wars you will love The Story of Asar, Aset and Heru.* Also, if you know the story of Jesus and Krishna you will discover than Ancient Egypt had a similar myth and that this myth carries important spiritual teachings for living a fruitful and fulfilling life. This book may be used along with *The Parents Guide To The Asarian Resurrection Myth: How to Teach Yourself and Your Child the Principles of Universal Mystical Religion.* The guide provides some background to the Asarian Resurrection myth and it also gives insight into the mystical teachings contained in it which you may introduce to your child. It is designed for parents who wish to grow spiritually with their children and it serves as an introduction for those who would like to study the Asarian Resurrection Myth in depth and to practice its teachings. 41 pages 8.5" X 11"   ISBN: 1-884564-31-3 $12.95

25.   THE PARENTS GUIDE TO THE AUSARIAN RESURRECTION MYTH: How to Teach Yourself and Your Child the Principles of Universal Mystical Religion.   This insightful manual brings for the timeless wisdom of the ancient through the Ancient Egyptian myth of Asar, Aset and Heru and the mystical teachings contained in it for parents who want to guide their children to understand and practice the teachings of mystical spirituality. This manual may be used with the children's storybook *The Story of Asar, Aset and Heru* by Dr. Muata Abhaya Ashby. 5.5"x 8.5"   ISBN: 1-884564-30-5 $14.95

26.   HEALING THE CRIMINAL HEART BOOK 1 Introduction to Maat Philosophy, Yoga and Spiritual Redemption Through the Path of Virtue   Who is a criminal? Is there such a thing as a criminal heart? What is the source of evil and sinfulness and is there any way to rise above it? Is there redemption for those who have committed sins, even the worst crimes?   Ancient Egyptian mystical psychology holds important answers to these questions. Over ten thousand years ago mystical psychologists, the Sages of Ancient Egypt, studied

Healing the Criminal Heart

and charted the human mind and spirit and laid out a path which will lead to spiritual redemption, prosperity and Enlightenment. This introductory volume brings forth the teachings of the Asarian Resurrection, the most important myth of Ancient Egypt, with relation to the faults of human existence: anger, hatred, greed, lust, animosity, discontent, ignorance, egoism jealousy, bitterness, and a myriad of psycho-spiritual ailments which keep a human being in a state of negativity and adversity. 5.5"x 8.5"   ISBN: 1-884564-17-8 $15.95

27.   THEATER & DRAMA OF THE ANCIENT EGYPTIAN MYSTERIES: Featuring the Ancient Egyptian stage play-"The Enlightenment of Hathor' Based on an Ancient Egyptian Drama, The original Theater -Mysticism of the Temple of Hetheru $14.95   By Dr. Muata Ashby

28.   GUIDE TO PRINT ON DEMAND: SELF-PUBLISH FOR PROFIT, SPIRITUAL FULFILLMENT AND SERVICE TO HUMANITY Everyone asks us how we produced so many books in such a short time. Here are the secrets to writing and producing books that uplift humanity and how to get them printed for a fraction of the regular cost. Anyone can become an author even if they have limited funds. All that is necessary is the willingness to learn how the printing and book business work and the desire to follow the special instructions given here for preparing your manuscript format. Then you take your work directly to the non-traditional companies who can produce your books for less than the traditional book printer can. ISBN: 1-884564-40-2 $16.95 U. S.

29.   Egyptian Mysteries: Vol. 1, Shetaut Neter ISBN: 1-884564-41-0 $19.99 What are the Mysteries? For thousands of years the spiritual tradition of Ancient Egypt, S*hetaut Neter,* "The Egyptian Mysteries," "The Secret Teachings," have fascinated, tantalized and amazed the world. At one time exalted and recognized as the highest culture of the world, by Africans, Europeans, Asiatics, Hindus, Buddhists and other cultures of the ancient world, in time it was shunned by the emerging orthodox world religions. Its temples desecrated, its philosophy maligned, its tradition spurned, its philosophy dormant in the mystical *Medu Neter*, the mysterious hieroglyphic texts which hold the secret symbolic meaning that has scarcely been discerned up to now. What are the secrets of *Nehast* {spiritual awakening and emancipation, resurrection}. More than just a literal translation, this volume is for awakening to the secret code *Shetitu* of the teaching which was not deciphered by Egyptologists, nor could be understood by ordinary spiritualists. This book is a reinstatement of the original science made available for our times, to the reincarnated followers of Ancient Egyptian culture and the prospect of spiritual freedom to break the bonds of *Khemn,* "ignorance," and slavery to evil forces: *Sâaa* .

30.   EGYPTIAN MYSTERIES VOL 2: Dictionary of Gods and Goddesses ISBN: 1-884564-23-2 $21.95 This book is about the mystery of neteru, the gods and goddesses of Ancient Egypt (Kamit, Kemet). Neteru means "Gods and

Goddesses." But the Neterian teaching of Neteru represents more than the usual limited modern day concept of "divinities" or "spirits." The Neteru of Kamit are also metaphors, cosmic principles and vehicles for the enlightening teachings of Shetaut Neter (Ancient Egyptian-African Religion). Actually they are the elements for one of the most advanced systems of spirituality ever conceived in human history. Understanding the concept of neteru provides a firm basis for spiritual evolution and the pathway for viable culture, peace on earth and a healthy human society.   Why is it important to have gods and goddesses in our lives? In order for spiritual evolution to be possible, once a human being has accepted that there is existence after death and there is a transcendental being who exists beyond time and space knowledge, human beings need a connection to that which transcends the ordinary experience of human life in time and space and a means to understand the transcendental reality beyond the mundane reality.

31.   EGYPTIAN MYSTERIES VOL. 3 The Priests and Priestesses of Ancient Egypt ISBN: 1-884564-53-4 $22.95 This volume details the path of Neterian priesthood, the joys, challenges and rewards of advanced Neterian life, the teachings that allowed the priests and priestesses to manage the most long lived civilization in human history and how that path can be adopted today; for those who want to tread the path of the Clergy of Shetaut Neter.

32.   THE KING OF EGYPT: The Struggle of Good and Evil for Control of the World and The Human Soul ISBN 1-8840564-44-5 $18.95   This volume contains a novelized version of the Asarian Resurrection myth that is based on the actual scriptures presented in the Book Asarian Religion (old name – Resurrecting Osiris). This volume is prepared in the form of a screenplay and can be easily adapted to be used as a stage play. Spiritual seeking is a mythic journey that has many emotional highs and lows, ecstasies and depressions, victories and frustrations. This is the War of Life that is played out in the myth as the struggle of Heru and Set and those are mythic characters that represent the human Higher and Lower self. How to understand the war and emerge victorious in the journey o life? The ultimate victory and fulfillment can be experienced, which is not changeable or lost in time. The purpose of myth is to convey the wisdom of life through the story of divinities who show the way to overcome the challenges and foibles of life. In this volume the feelings and emotions of the characters of the myth have been highlighted to show the deeply rich texture of the Ancient Egyptian myth. This myth contains deep spiritual teachings and insights into the nature of self, of God and the mysteries of life and the means to discover the true meaning of life and thereby achieve the true purpose of life. To become victorious in the battle of life means to become the King (or Queen) of Egypt.Have you seen movies like The Lion King, Hamlet, The Odyssey, or The Little Buddha? These have been some of the most popular movies in modern times. The Sema Institute of Yoga is dedicated to researching and presenting the wisdom and culture of ancient Africa. The Script is designed

to be produced as a motion picture but may be addapted for the theater as well. $19.95   copyright 1998 By Dr. Muata Ashby

33.   AFRICAN DIONYSUS: FROM EGYPT TO GREECE: The Kamitan Origins of Greek Culture and Religion ISBN: 1-884564-47-X $24.95 U.S. FROM EGYPT TO GREECE   This insightful manual is a reference to Ancient Egyptian mythology and philosophy and its correlation to what later became known as Greek and Rome mythology and philosophy. It outlines the basic tenets of the mythologies and shoes the ancient origins of Greek culture in Ancient Egypt. This volume also documents the origins of the Greek alphabet in Egypt as well as Greek religion, myth and philosophy of the gods and goddesses from Egypt from the myth of Atlantis and archaic period with the Minoans to the Classical period. This volume also acts as a resource for Colleges students who would like to set up fraternities and sororities based on the original Ancient Egyptian principles of Sheti and Maat philosophy. ISBN: 1-884564-47-X $22.95 U.S.

34.   THE FORTY TWO   PRECEPTS OF MAAT,   THE PHILOSOPHY OF RIGHTEOUS ACTION AND THE ANCIENT EGYPTIAN WISDOM TEXTS ADVANCED STUDIES This manual is designed for use with the 1998 Maat Philosophy Class conducted by Dr. Muata Ashby. This is a detailed study of Maat Philosophy. It contains a compilation of the 42 laws or precepts of Maat and the corresponding principles which they represent along with the teachings of the ancient Egyptian Sages relating to each. Maat philosophy was the basis of Ancient Egyptian society and government as well as the heart of Ancient Egyptian myth and spirituality. Maat is at once a goddess, a cosmic force and a living social doctrine, which promotes social harmony and thereby paves the way for spiritual evolution in all levels of society. ISBN: 1-884564-48-8 $16.95 U.S.

Music Based on the Prt M Hru and other Kemetic Texts

Available on Compact Disc $14.99 and Audio Cassette $9.99

Adorations to the Goddess

Music for Worship of the Goddess

**NEW Egyptian Yoga Music CD
by Sehu Maa
Ancient Egyptian Music CD**
Instrumental Music played on reproductions of Ancient Egyptian
Instruments– Ideal for <u>meditation</u> and
reflection on the Divine and for the practice of spiritual programs and
<u>Yoga exercise sessions.</u>

©1999 By Muata Ashby
CD $14.99 –

MERIT'S INSPIRATION
NEW Egyptian Yoga Music CD

Healing the Criminal Heart

by Sehu Maa
Ancient Egyptian Music CD
Instrumental Music played on
reproductions of Ancient Egyptian Instruments– Ideal for <u>meditation</u> and
reflection on the Divine and for the practice of spiritual programs and
<u>Yoga exercise sessions.</u>
©1999 By
Muata Ashby
CD $14.99 –
UPC# 761527100429

ANORATIONS TO RA AND HETHERU
NEW Egyptian Yoga Music CD
By Sehu Maa (Muata Ashby)
Based on the Words of Power of Ra and HetHeru
played on reproductions of Ancient Egyptian Instruments **Ancient**
Egyptian Instruments used: Voice, Clapping, Nefer Lute, Tar Drum,
Sistrums, Cymbals – The Chants, Devotions, Rhythms and Festive
Songs Of the Neteru – Ideal for meditation, and devotional singing and
dancing.
©1999 By Muata Ashby
CD $14.99 –
UPC# 761527100221

Healing the Criminal Heart

SONGS TO ASAR ASET AND HERU
NEW
Egyptian Yoga Music CD
By Sehu Maa

played on reproductions of Ancient Egyptian Instruments– The Chants,
Devotions, Rhythms and
Festive Songs Of the Neteru - Ideal for meditation, and devotional singing and dancing.

Based on the Words of Power of Asar (Asar), Aset (Aset) and Heru (Heru) Om Asar Aset Heru is the third in a series of musical explorations of the Kemetic (Ancient Egyptian) tradition of music. Its ideas are based on the Ancient Egyptian Religion of Asar, Aset and Heru and it is designed for listening, meditation and worship. ©1999 By Muata Ashby
CD $14.99 –
UPC# 761527100122

HAARI OM: ANCIENT EGYPT MEETS INDIA IN MUSIC
NEW Music CD
By Sehu Maa

The Chants, Devotions, Rhythms and

Healing the Criminal Heart

Festive Songs Of the Ancient Egypt and India, harmonized and played on reproductions of ancient instruments along with modern instruments and beats. Ideal for meditation, and devotional singing and dancing.

Haari Om is the fourth in a series of musical explorations of the Kemetic (Ancient Egyptian) and Indian traditions of music, chanting and devotional spiritual practice. Its ideas are based on the Ancient Egyptian Yoga spirituality and Indian Yoga spirituality.

©1999 By Muata Ashby

CD $14.99 –

UPC# 761527100528

RA AKHU: THE GLORIOUS LIGHT
NEW
Egyptian Yoga Music CD
By Sehu Maa

The fifth collection of original music compositions based on the Teachings and Words of The Trinity, the God Asar and the Goddess Nebethet, the Divinity Aten, the God Heru, and the Special Meditation Hekau or Words of Power of Ra from the Ancient Egyptian Tomb of Seti I and more... played on reproductions of Ancient Egyptian Instruments and modern instruments - Ancient Egyptian Instruments used: Voice, Clapping, Nefer Lute, Tar Drum, Sistrums, Cymbals

— The Chants, Devotions, Rhythms and Festive Songs Of the Neteru – Ideal for meditation, and devotional singing and dancing.

©1999 By Muata Ashby

CD $14.99 –

UPC# 761527100825

GLORIES OF THE DIVINE MOTHER
Based on the hieroglyphic text of the worship of Goddess Net.
The Glories of The Great Mother
©2000 Muata Ashby
CD $14.99 UPC# 761527101129`

Healing the Criminal Heart

Order Form

Telephone orders: Call Toll Free: 1(305) 378-6253. Have your AMEX, Optima, Visa or MasterCard ready.

Fax orders: 1-(305) 378-6253   E-MAIL ADDRESS: Semayoga@aol.com

Postal Orders: Sema Institute of Yoga, P.O. Box 570459, Miami, Fl. 33257. USA.

Please send the following books and / or tapes.

ITEM

_____Cost $_____

_____Cost $_____

_____Cost $_____

_____Cost $_____

_____Cost $_____

Total $_____

Name:_____

Physical Address:_____

City:_____ State:_____ Zip:_____

Sales tax: Please add 6.5% for books shipped to Florida addresses

_____Shipping: $6.50 for first book and .50¢ for each additional

_____Shipping: Outside US $5.00 for first book and $3.00 for each additional

_____Payment:_____

_____Check -Include Driver License #:

_____

_____Credit card:_____ Visa, _____ MasterCard, _____ Optima,

_____ AMEX.

Card number:_____

Name on card:_____ Exp. date:_____ /_____

Copyright 1995-2005 Dr. R. Muata Abhaya Ashby
Sema Institute of Yoga
P.O.Box 570459, Miami, Florida, 33257
(305) 378-6253 Fax: (305) 378-6253

Lightning Source UK Ltd.
Milton Keynes UK
UKOW050152161111

182106UK00001B/103/A